THE EMPIRE STRIKES BACK

™

SCRIPT FACSIMILE

PUBLISHED BY DEL REY BOOKS:

Art of Star Wars: A New Hope

Art of Star Wars: The Empire Strikes Back

Art of Star Wars: Return of the Jedi

Star Wars: A New Hope
The National Public Radio Dramatization

Star Wars: The Empire Strikes Back
The National Public Radio Dramatization

Star Wars: Return of the Jedi
The National Public Radio Dramatization

Star Wars: The Annotated Screenplays

A Guide to the Star Wars Universe

Star Wars Encyclopedia

Star Wars: A New Hope
The Illustrated Screenplay

Star Wars: The Empire Strikes Back
The Illustrated Screenplay

Star Wars: Return of the Jedi
The Illustrated Screenplay

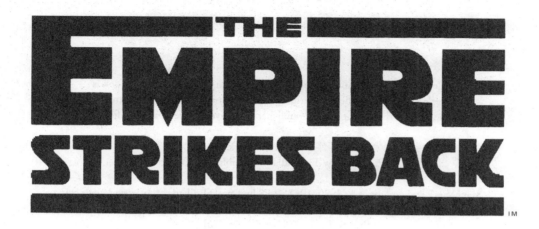

THE EMPIRE STRIKES BACK

SCRIPT FACSIMILE

STORY BY

GEORGE LUCAS

ORIGINAL SCREENPLAY BY

LEIGH BRACKETT AND
LAWRENCE KASDAN

THE BALLANTINE PUBLISHING GROUP

NEW YORK

A Del Rey® Book
Published by The Ballantine Publishing Group

Star Wars® and copyright © 1980, 1997, 1998 by Lucasfilm Ltd. ™, title, and character
and place names protected by all applicable trademark laws.
All Rights Reserved. Used Under Authorization.

All rights reserved under International and Pan-American Copyright
Conventions. Published in the United States by The Ballantine Publishing
Group, a division of Random House, Inc., New York, and simultaneously in
Canada by Random House of Canada Limited, Toronto. Originally published
in different form in *Star Wars: The Empire Strikes Back Illustrated Screenplay* and
Star Wars: The Annotated Screenplays.

http://www.randomhouse.com/delrey/

Library of Congress Catalog Card Number: 98-96427

ISBN 0-345-42081-0

Cover design by Min Choi

Manufactured in the United States of America

First Edition: November 1998

10   9   8   7   6   5   4   3   2   1

Dear Reader:

In 1997 Lucasfilm Ltd. released all three of
the original Star Wars films as the Star Wars
Trilogy Special Edition. Filmmaker George Lucas
was afforded the extraordinary opportunity to
complete these landmark films as he had
originally envisioned them, and to restore each
to the highest visual and sound quality
available.

With the Special Edition releases, Lucas was
able to take advantage of two decades of
advances in filmmaking technology that had begun
with the original Star Wars: A New Hope and had
been spearheaded by the special effects wizards
of Industrial Light & Magic. And in doing so,
he was able to get the ball rolling on
advancements that very likely play a major role
in the next Star Wars trilogy, beginning with
Episode I in 1999.

Before the Special Edition trilogy could be
executed, the Lucasfilm creative team had to
work closely with Lucas to identify each scene
that would be created or recovered, each
special effect that would be added or improved
upon. Then they had to fit each scene into the
original film, so the result would flow
seamlessly across the theater screen.

What you hold in your hands is a first: the
original movie script, with the Special Edition
scene descriptions inserted. This script
represents the complete screenplay. As a bonus,
you also have a photo gallery that shows some
of the end results, including photo stills that
are being published for the very first time.

We hope you enjoy this book as much as we
enjoyed having a part in its creation.

The Editors:
Sue Rostoni
Steve Saffel

A long time ago in a galaxy far, far
away . . . .

A vast sea of stars serves as the backdrop for the main
title, followed by a roll-up which crawls into infinity.

It is a dark time for the Rebellion. Although
the Death Star has been destroyed, Imperial
troops have driven the Rebel forces from
their hidden base and pursued them across the
galaxy.

Evading the dreaded Imperial Starfleet, a
group of freedom fighters led by Luke
Skywalker has established a new secret base
on the remote ice world of Hoth.

The evil lord Darth Vader, obsessed with
finding young Skywalker, has dispatched
thousands of remote probes into the far
reaches of space . . .

(CONTINUED)

EXT. GALAXY — PLANET HOTH

A Star Destroyer moves through space, releasing Imperial probe
robots from its underside.

One of these probes zooms toward the planet Hoth and lands on its
ice-covered surface. An explosion marks the point of impact.

EXT. HOTH — METEORITE CRATER — SNOW PLAIN — DAY

A weird mechanical sound rises above the whining of the wind. A
strange probe robot, with several extended sensors, emerges from the
smoke-shrouded crater. The ominous mechanical probe floats across
the snow plain and disappears into the distance.

EXT. PLAIN OF HOTH — DAY

A small figure gallops across the windswept ice slope. The bundled
rider is mounted on a large gray snow lizard, a tauntaun. Curving
plumes of snow rise from beneath the speeding paws of the two-legged
beast.

The rider gallops up a slope and reins his lizard to a stop. Pulling
off his protective goggles, Luke Skywalker notices something in the
sky. He takes a pair of electrobinoculars from his utility belt and
through them sees smoke rising from where the probe robot has
crashed.

The wind whips at Luke's fur-lined cap and he activates a comlink
transmitter. His tauntaun shifts and moans nervously beneath him.

                    LUKE
          (into comlink) Echo Three to Echo Seven. Han,
          old buddy, do you read me?

After a little static a familiar voice is heard.

                    HAN
          (over comlink) Loud and clear, kid. What's up?

                    LUKE
          (into comlink) Well, I finished my circle. I
          don't pick up any life readings.

(CONTINUED)

CONTINUED:

                           HAN
          (over comlink) There isn't enough life on
          this ice cube to fill a space cruiser. The
          sensors are placed. I'm going back.

                           LUKE
          (into comlink) Right. I'll see you shortly.
          There's a meteorite that hit the ground near
          here. I want to check it out. It won't
          take long.

Luke clicks off his transmitter and reins back on his nervous
lizard. He pats the beast on the head to calm it.

                           LUKE
          Hey, steady girl. What's the matter? You
          smell something?

Luke takes a small device from his belt and starts to adjust it when
suddenly a large shadow falls over him from behind. He hears a
monstrous howl and turns to see an eleven-foot-tall shape towering
over him. It is a wampa ice creature, lunging at him ferociously.

                           LUKE
          Aaargh!

Luke grabs for his pistol, but is hit flat in the face by a huge
white claw. He falls unconscious into the snow and in a moment the
terrified screams of the tauntaun are cut short by the horrible snap
of a neck being broken.

The wampa ice creature grabs Luke by one ankle and drags him away
across the frozen plain.

EXT. HOTH — REBEL BASE ENTRANCE — DAY

A stalwart figure rides his tauntaun up to the entrance of an
enormous ice cave.

INT. HOTH — REBEL BASE — MAIN HANGAR DECK

Rebel troopers rush about unloading supplies and otherwise securing
their new base. The rider, Han Solo, swings off his lizard and pulls
off his goggles.

He walks into the main hangar deck toward the Millennium Falcon,
which is parked among several fighters. Mechanics, R2 units, and
various other droids hurry about. Han stops at the Millennium Falcon
where his Wookiee copilot, Chewbacca, is welding on a central
lifter. Chewie stops his work and lifts his face shield, growling an
irritated greeting to his boss.

                                                        (CONTINUED)

CONTINUED:

                              HAN

          Chewie!

The Wookiee grumbles a reply.

                              HAN

          All right, don't lose your temper. I'll come
          right back and give you a hand.

Chewbacca puts his mask back on and returns to his welding as Han
leaves.

INT. HOTH — REBEL BASE — COMMAND CENTER

A makeshift command center has been set up in a blasted area of
thick ice. The low-ceilinged room is a beehive of activity.
Controllers, troopers, and droids move about setting up electronic
equipment and monitoring radar signals.

General Rieekan straightens up from a console at Han's approach.

                              RIEEKAN

          Solo?

                              HAN

          No sign of life out there, General. The
          sensors are in place. You'll know if anything
          comes around.

                              RIEEKAN

          Commander Skywalker reported in yet?

                              HAN

          No. He's checking out a meteorite that hit
          near him.

                              RIEEKAN

          (indicates radar screen) With all the meteor
          activity in this system, it's going to be
          difficult to spot approaching ships.

Taking a deep breath, Han blurts out what is on his mind.

                              HAN

          General, I've got to leave. I can't stay
          anymore.

Princess Leia, standing at a console nearby, is dressed in a short
white combat jacket and pants. Her hair is braided and tied across
her head in a Nordic fashion. She overhears their conversation and
seems somewhat distressed.

                              RIEEKAN

          I'm sorry to hear that.

                                                        (CONTINUED)

CONTINUED:

> HAN
>
> Well, there's a price on my head. If I don't
> pay off Jabba the Hutt, I'm a dead man.
>
> RIEEKAN
>
> A death mark's not an easy thing to live
> with. You're a good fighter, Solo. I hate to
> lose you.
>
> HAN
>
> Thank you, General.

He turns to Leia as Rieekan moves away.

> HAN
>
> (with feeling) Well, Your Highness, I guess
> this is it.
>
> LEIA
>
> That's right.

Leia is angry. Han sees she has no warmth to offer him. He shakes
his head and adopts a sarcastic tone.

> HAN
>
> (coolly) Well, don't get all mushy on me. So
> long, Princess.

Han walks away into the quiet corridor adjoining the command center.
Leia stews a moment, then hurries after him.

INT. HOTH — REBEL BASE — ICE CORRIDOR

> LEIA
>
> Han!

Han stops in the corridor and turns to face Leia.

> HAN
>
> Yes, Your Highnessness?
>
> LEIA
>
> I thought you had decided to stay.
>
> HAN
>
> Well, the bounty hunter we ran into on Ord
> Mantell changed my mind.
>
> LEIA
>
> Han, we need you!
>
> HAN
>
> We?
>
> LEIA
>
> Yes.

(CONTINUED)

CONTINUED:

                    HAN
        Oh, what about <u>you</u> need?

                    LEIA
        (mystified) I need? I don't know what you're
        talking about.

                    HAN
        (shakes his head, fed up) You probably don't.

                    LEIA
        And what precisely am I supposed to know?

                    HAN
        Come on! You want me to stay because of the
        way you feel about me.

                    LEIA
        Yes. You're a great help to us. You're a
        natural leader . . .

                    HAN
        No! That's not it. Come on. Aahhh — uh-huh!
        Come on.

Leia stares at him, understands, then laughs.

                    LEIA
        You're imagining things.

                    HAN
        Am I? Then why are you following me? Afraid I was
        going to leave without giving you a good-bye kiss?

                    LEIA
        I'd just as soon kiss a Wookiee.

                    HAN
        I can arrange that. You could use a good kiss!

Angrily, Han strides down the corridor as Leia stares after him.

INT. HOTH — REBEL BASE — ANOTHER ICE CORRIDOR

A familiar stream of beeps and whistles heralds the approach of
Artoo-Detoo and See-Threepio, who appear around a corner and move
along an ice wall toward the main hangar.

                    THREEPIO
        Don't try to blame me. I didn't ask you to
        turn on the thermal heater. I merely
        commented that it was freezing in the
        princess's chamber. But it's <u>supposed</u> to be
        freezing. How are we going to dry out all her
        clothes? I really don't know.

                                            (CONTINUED)

CONTINUED:

Artoo beeps a stream of protesting whistles.

                    THREEPIO
          Oh, switch off.

INT. HOTH — REBEL BASE — MAIN HANGAR DECK

The two robots stop at Han Solo's space freighter. Han and Chewie
are still struggling with their central lifters.

                    HAN
          (to Chewie) Why do you take this apart now?
          I'm trying to get us out of here and you pull
          both of these.

Chewie grumbles in irritation.

                    THREEPIO
          Excuse me, sir.

                    HAN
          (to Chewie) Put them back together right now.

                    THREEPIO
          Might I have a word with you, please?

                    HAN
          What do you want?

                    THREEPIO
          Well, it's Princess Leia, sir. She's been
          trying to get you on the communicator.

                    HAN
          I turned it off. I don't want to talk to her.

                    THREEPIO
          Oh. Well, Princess Leia is wondering about
          Master Luke. He hasn't come back yet. She
          doesn't know where he is.

                    HAN
          I don't know where he is.

                    THREEPIO
          Nobody knows where he is.

                    HAN
          What do you mean, "nobody knows"?

Han glances at the fading light at the entrance of the ice cave as
night slowly begins to fall on the planet.

                    THREEPIO
          Well, uh, you see . . .

Han jumps down off the lift, as Threepio follows him.

(CONTINUED)

CONTINUED:

                    HAN
          Deck Officer. Deck Officer!

                    THREEPIO
          Excuse me, sir. Might I inqu- . . .

Han abruptly puts his hand over Threepio's mouth as the deck officer
approaches.

                    DECK OFFICER
          Yes, sir?

                    HAN
          Do you know where Commander Skywalker is?

                    DECK OFFICER
          I haven't seen him. It's possible he came in
          through the south entrance.

                    HAN
          It's possible? Why don't you go find out? It's
          getting dark out there.

                    DECK OFFICER
          Yes, sir.

The deck officer leaves hurriedly, as Han takes his hand off
Threepio's mouth.

                    THREEPIO
          Excuse me, sir. Might I inquire what's
          going on?

                    HAN
          Why not?

                    THREEPIO
          Impossible man. Come along, Artoo, let's find
          Princess Leia. Between ourselves, I think
          Master Luke is in considerable danger.

INT. HOTH — REBEL BASE — MAIN ICE TUNNEL

The deck officer and his assistant hurry toward Han as he enters the
tunnel.

                    DECK OFFICER
          Sir, Commander Skywalker hasn't come in
          through the south entrance. He might have
          forgotten to check in.

                    HAN
          Not likely. Are the speeders ready?

                                        (CONTINUED)

CONTINUED:

                    DECK OFFICER
          Not yet. We're having some trouble adapting
          them to the cold.

                    HAN
          Then we'll have to go out on tauntauns.

                    DECK OFFICER
          Sir, the temperature's dropping too rapidly.

                    HAN
          That's right. And my friend's out in it.

                    ASSISTANT OFFICER
          I'll cover sector twelve. Have com-control
          set screen alpha.

Han pushes through the troops and mounts a tauntaun.

                    DECK OFFICER
          Your tauntaun'll freeze before you reach the
          first marker.

                    HAN
          Then I'll see you in hell!

Han maneuvers his mount out of the cave and races into the dark and
bitter night.

EXT. HOTH — ICE GORGE — DUSK

The jagged face of a huge ice wall sits gloomily in the dim twilight ←Start
of a Hoth day. Luke hangs upside down, ankles frozen into icy   replace-
stalactites, his extended arms within a foot of the snow floor. One   ment
side of his face is covered in a dried mask of frozen blood. He   scene here
opens his eyes as a chilling moan of the hideous ice creature echoes   from page
off the gorge walls. Luke pulls himself up, grabs hold of his   10A for
ankles, and futilely tries to unfasten the thongs.   the
                                                                       Special
Exhausted, he drops back into his hanging position. As he hangs   Edition
there, he spies his lightsaber lying near a pile of his discarded
gear, about three feet out of reach.

He focuses on the saber and, as his hand strains toward the weapon,
he squeezes his eyes tight in concentration.

Just as the ice creature looms over Luke, the lightsaber jumps into
Luke's hand.

The young warrior instantly ignites his sword, swings up, and cuts
himself loose from the ice. He flops to the snow in a heap. The
startled creature moves back, his giant yellow eyes blinking. Luke
scrambles to his feet. He swings his lightsaber and the beast   ←End
screams in pain.   replace-
                                                                     ment
                                                                     scene
                                                                     Special
                                                                     Edition

EXT. HOTH — ENTRANCE TO ICE GORGE — DUSK

Luke staggers out of the gorge into the dark and snowy twilight.
Weak and exhausted, he stumbles down a snow bank.

EXT. HOTH — SNOW PLAIN — DUSK

A small, lone figure riding a tauntaun races through the hostile
vastness of snow and cold. As it runs, the tauntaun's legs kick up
large clouds of snow and ice into the snowy air.

EXT. HOTH — OUTSIDE ICE HANGAR — DUSK

Artoo stands in the falling snow, beeping worriedly. Threepio moves
stiffly over to him.

> THREEPIO
> You must come along now, Artoo. There's
> really nothing more we can do. And my joints
> are freezing up.

Artoo beeps, long and low.

> THREEPIO
> Don't say things like that! Of course we'll
> see Master Luke again. He'll be quite all
> right, you'll see. (to himself) Stupid little
> short-circuit. He'll be quite all right.

Threepio turns to go back inside the main hangar as Artoo mournfully
keeps his vigil.

EXT. HOTH — SNOWDRIFT — DUSK

The wind is blowing quite strong now. Luke struggles to stay
upright, but a blast of freezing snow knocks him over. He struggles
to get up, but he can't. The young warrior from Tatooine drags
himself a couple of feet and then collapses.

INT. REBEL BASE — MAIN HANGAR DECK — ENTRANCE — NIGHT

Princess Leia stands inside the dark entrance to the Rebel base,
waiting for a sign of the two Rebel heroes. She shivers in the cold
wind as, nearby, Chewie sits with his head in his hands. In the
background, Artoo and Threepio move through the doors.

A Rebel lieutenant moves to Major Derlin, an officer keeping watch
with the princess.

(CONTINUED)

SPECIAL EDITION INSERT TO PAGE 9

The jagged face of a huge ice wall sits gloomily in the dim twilight of a Hoth day. Luke hangs upside down, ankles frozen into icy stalactites, his extended arms within a foot of the snow floor. One side of his face is covered in a dried mask of frozen blood. He opens his eyes as a chilling moan of the hideous ice creature echoes off the gorge walls. The wampa creature is in the ice cave eating what appears to be carrion. It turns in Luke's direction and growls, then continues its meal. Luke pulls himself up, grabs hold of his ankles, and futilely tries to unfasten the thongs.

Exhausted, he drops back into his hanging position. The wampa continues eating, tearing away huge bites of carrion. As Luke hangs there, he spies his lightsaber stuck in the snow, about three feet out of reach.

Luke's motion distracts the creature. The wampa stops eating, stands upright, growls, and starts toward Luke. Finally, using the Force, Luke frees his lightsaber from the snow and it jumps to his hand. The wampa continues to approach. Luke cuts his feet loose from the ice and drops down to the snow, sword blazing. The creature nears. Luke scrambles to his feet and swings his lightsaber, and the beast's right arm is left lying in the snow. The wampa screams in pain, and Luke flees.

CONTINUED:

> LIEUTENANT
> Sir, all the patrols are in. There's still no
> contact from Skywalker or Solo.

> THREEPIO
> Mistress Leia, Artoo says he's been quite
> unable to pick up any signals, although he
> does admit that his own range is far too weak
> to abandon all hope.

Leia nods an acknowledgment, but she is lost in thought.

> DERLIN
> Your Highness, there's nothing more we can do
> tonight. The shield doors must be closed.

He turns to the lieutenant.

> DERLIN
> Close the doors.

> LIEUTENANT
> Yes, sir.

The lieutenant walks away. Chewie lets out a long, mournful howl,
somewhat like a coyote. At the same moment, Artoo begins a complex
series of efficient beeps.

> THREEPIO
> Artoo says the chances of survival are seven
> hundred seventy-five . . . to one.

Leia stands praying to herself as the huge metal doors slam across
the entrances of the ice cave. The loud booms echo throughout the
huge cavern. Chewie lets out another suffering howl.

> THREEPIO
> Actually, Artoo has been known to make
> mistakes . . . from time to time. Oh, dear,
> oh, dear. Don't worry about Master Luke. I'm
> sure he'll be all right. He's quite clever,
> you know . . . for a human being.

EXT. HOTH — SNOWDRIFT — DUSK

Luke lies face down in the snow, nearly unconscious. Slowly he looks
up and sees Ben Kenobi, barely visible through the blowing snow. It
is hard to tell if Kenobi is real or a hallucination.

> BEN
> Luke . . . Luke.

> LUKE
> (weakly) Ben?

(CONTINUED)

CONTINUED:

> BEN
> You will go to the Dagobah system.

> LUKE
> Dagobah system?

> BEN
> There you will learn from Yoda, the Jedi
> Master who instructed me.

The image of Ben fades, revealing a lone tauntaun rider approaching from the windswept horizon.

> LUKE
> (groaning faintly) Ben . . . Ben.

Luke drops into unconsciousness.

Han pulls up and leaps off his mount. He hurries to his snow-covered friend, cradling him in his arms. Han's tauntaun lets out a low, pitiful bellow. But Han's concern is with Luke, and he shakes him urgently.

> HAN
> Luke! Luke! Don't do this, Luke. Come on,
> give me a sign here.

Luke doesn't respond. Han begins frantically rubbing and slapping Luke's unconscious face. As he starts to lift the youth, Han hears a rasping sound behind him. He turns, just in time to see his tauntaun stagger and then fall over into the snow.

Han carries Luke to the moaning beast. Then, with a final groan, the tauntaun expires.

> HAN
> Not much time.

He pushes Luke's inert form against the belly of the dead beast.

> LUKE
> (moaning) Ben . . . Ben . . .

> HAN
> Hang on, kid.

> LUKE
> Dagobah system . . .

Han ignites Luke's saber and cuts the beast from head to toe. He quickly tosses its steaming innards into the snow, then lifts Luke's inert form and stuffs him inside the carcass.

> HAN
> (reeling from the odor) Whew . . .

> LUKE
> Dagobah . . .

(CONTINUED)

CONTINUED:

                          HAN
          This may smell bad, kid . . .

                          LUKE
          (moaning) Yoda . . .

                          HAN
          . . . but it will keep you warm . . . till I
          get the shelter built. (struggling to get
          Luke inside the carcass) Ooh . . . I thought
          they smelled bad on the outside!

The wind has picked up considerably, making it difficult to move.
Han removes a pack from the dead creature's back, taking out a
shelter container. He begins to set up what can only be a pitiful
protection against a bitter Hoth night.

EXT. HOTH — SNOWDRIFT — DAWN

Four snub-nosed armored snowspeeders race across the white
landscape.

INT. SNOWSPEEDER — COCKPIT

There is only one pilot, Zev, in the enclosed two-man craft. He
concentrates on the scopes which ring his cockpit. He hears a low
beep from one of his monitors.

                          ZEV
          (into transmitter) Echo Base . . . I've got
          something! Not much, but it could be a life
          form.

EXT. HOTH — SNOWDRIFT

The small craft banks and makes a slow arc, then races off in a new
direction.

INT. SNOWSPEEDER — COCKPIT

The pilot switches over to a new transmitter.

                          ZEV
          (into transmitter) This is Rogue Two. This is
          Rogue Two. Captain Solo, do you copy?
          Commander Skywalker, do you copy? This is
          Rogue Two.

There is a sharp crackle of static, then a faint voice.

                                                    (CONTINUED)

CONTINUED:

                       HAN
       (filtered over Zev's receiver) Good morning.
       Nice of you guys to drop by.

                       ZEV
       (switching transmitters) Echo Base . . . this
       is Rogue Two. I found them. Repeat, I found
       them.

EXT. HOTH — SNOWDRIFT — DAY

The small shelter Han has set up is covered with snow on the windward side. A makeshift antenna rests gingerly on top of the snowdrift. Han spots Zev's snowspeeder approaching in the distance, and begins waving frantically at the tiny craft.

INT. REBEL BASE — MEDICAL CENTER

Strange robot surgeons adjust a mass of electronic equipment. A switch is thrown and a sudden blinding flash obscures Luke in a bacta tank filled with a thick, gelatinous slime. He begins to thrash about, raving in his delirium.

INT. REBEL BASE — MEDICAL CENTER — RECOVERY ROOM

Luke sits up in a recovery-room bed, weak but smiling. His face shows terrible wounds from the wampa's attack. Threepio and Artoo enter the room.

                  THREEPIO
       Master Luke, sir, it's so good to see you
       fully functional again.

Artoo beeps his good wishes.

                  THREEPIO
       Artoo expresses his relief, also.

Han and Chewie make their entrance. The Wookiee growls a greeting.

                     HAN
       How are you feeling, kid? You don't look so
       bad to me. In fact, you look strong enough to
       pull the ears off a gundark.

                    LUKE
       Thanks to you.

                     HAN
       That's two you owe me, junior.

(CONTINUED)

CONTINUED:

Han turns as Leia enters the room. He looks at her with a big, devilish grin.

                    HAN
        Well, Your Worship, looks like you managed to
        keep me around for a little while longer.

                    LEIA
        (haughtily) I had nothing to do with it.
        General Rieekan thinks it's dangerous for any
        ships to leave the system until we've
        activated the energy shield.

                    HAN
        That's a good story. I think you just can't
        bear to let a gorgeous guy like me out of
        your sight.

                    LEIA
        I don't know where you get your delusions,
        laser brain.

Chewie is amused; he laughs in his manner. Han, enjoying himself, regards Chewie good-humoredly.

                    HAN
        Laugh it up, fuzzball. But you didn't see us
        alone in the south passage.

Luke sparks to this; he looks at Leia.

                    HAN
        She expressed her true feelings for me.

Leia is flushed, eyes darting between Luke and Han.

                    LEIA
        My . . . ! Why, you stuck-up, . . . half-
        witted, . . . scruffy-looking . . . nerf-
        herder!

                    HAN
        Who's scruffy-looking? (to Luke) I must have
        hit pretty close to the mark to get her all
        riled up like that, huh, kid?

Leia looks vulnerable for a moment, then the mask falls again, and she focuses on Luke.

                    LEIA
        Why, I guess you don't know everything about
        women yet.

With that she leans over and kisses Luke on the lips. Then she turns on her heel and walks out, leaving everyone in the room slightly dumbstruck. With some smugness, Luke puts his hands behind his head and grins.

                                        (CONTINUED)

CONTINUED:

Suddenly, in the distance, the muffled sound of an alarm is heard.

                    ANNOUNCER
          (over loudspeaker) Headquarters personnel,
          report to command center.

The voice repeats the order and Han, Chewie, Artoo, and Threepio
hurry out of the room, bidding farewell to Luke.

                    HAN
          Take it easy.

                    THREEPIO
          Excuse us, please.

INT. HOTH — REBEL BASE — COMMAND CENTER

Rieekan looks up grimly from a console screen. He calls over to Leia
and Han.

                    RIEEKAN
          Princess . . . we have a visitor.

The group hurries over to Rieekan.

                    RIEEKAN
          We've picked up something outside the base in
          zone twelve, moving east.

                    SENIOR CONTROLLER
          It's metal.

                    LEIA
          Then it couldn't be one of those creatures
          that attacked Luke.

                    HAN
          It could be a speeder, one of ours.

                    SENIOR CONTROLLER
          No. Wait — there's something very weak coming
          through.

Threepio steps up to the control panel and listens intently to the
strange signal.

                    THREEPIO
          Sir, I am fluent in six million forms of
          communication. This signal is not used by the
          Alliance. It could be an Imperial code.

The transmission ends in static.

                    HAN
          It isn't friendly, whatever it is. Come on,
          Chewie, let's check it out.

                                        (CONTINUED)

CONTINUED:

                    RIEEKAN
      Send Rogues Ten and Eleven to station three-
      eight.

EXT. HOTH — SNOW PLAIN — DAY

The dark probe robot moves past the smoldering ruins of station three-eight and down a ridge toward the Rebel base. It raises a large antenna from the top of its head and begins to send out a piercing signal.

The probe droid has spotted Chewbacca who, not thirty feet away, has popped his head over a snow bank. Instantly, the probe robot swings around, its deadly ray ready to fire. But before it can get a shot off, it is hit from behind by a laser bolt, and explodes in a million pieces.

Han Solo replaces his blaster in its holster and peers intently at the smoldering remains of the Imperial probe.

INT. HOTH — REBEL BASE — COMMAND CENTER

Leia and Rieekan listen to Han on the comlink.

                    HAN
      (over comlink) Afraid there's not much left.

                    LEIA
      (into comlink) What was it?

                    HAN
      (over comlink) Droid of some kind. I didn't
      hit it that hard. It must have had a self-
      destruct.

                    LEIA
      (into comlink) An Imperial probe droid.

                    HAN
      (over comlink) It's a good bet the Empire
      knows we're here.

                    RIEEKAN
      We'd better start the evacuation.

EXT. SPACE — IMPERIAL FLEET

Darth Vader's Star Destroyer, larger and more awesome than the five Imperial Star Destroyers that surround it, sits in the vastness of space. The six huge ships are surrounded by a convoy of smaller spacecraft. TIE fighters dart to and fro.

INT. DARTH VADER'S STAR DESTROYER — BRIDGE — MAIN CONTROL DECK

Controllers working the vast complex of electronic controls hear ominous approaching footsteps and look up from their controls. The squat, evil-looking Admiral Ozzel and the young, powerfully built General Veers, who have been conferring near the front, also feel the approaching presence and turn toward it. Darth Vader, Lord of the Sith, enters like a chill wind. As Vader moves across the wide bridge, Captain Piett hurries up to Ozzel.

                    PIETT
          Admiral.

                    OZZEL
          Yes, Captain?

                    PIETT
          I think we've got something, sir. The report
          is only a fragment from a probe droid in
          the Hoth system, but it's the best lead
          we've had.

                    OZZEL
          (irritated) We have thousands of probe droids
          searching the galaxy. I want proof, not
          leads!

                    PIETT
          The visuals indicate life readings.

                    OZZEL
          It could mean anything. If we followed up
          every lead . . .

                    PIETT
          But, sir, the Hoth system is supposed to be
          devoid of human forms.

Vader moves to a large screen showing an image of the Rebel snow base. Rebel speeders can be seen approaching the base in the distance.

                    VADER
          You found something?

                    PIETT
          Yes, my lord.

                    VADER
          (studying the image on the console screen)
          That's it. The Rebels are there.

                    OZZEL
          My lord, there are so many uncharted settle-
          ments. It could be smugglers, it could
          be . . .

                                        (CONTINUED)

CONTINUED:

>   VADER
>   That is the system. And I'm sure Skywalker is
>   with them. Set your course for the Hoth
>   system. General Veers, prepare your men.

INT. HOTH — REBEL BASE — TRANSPORT BAY

A captain issues instructions to two of his men at the entrance to
the main transport bay. Several Rebel transports behind them are
being loaded by men carrying heavy boxes and moving quickly, but not
in panic.

>   REBEL CAPTAIN
>   Groups seven and ten will stay behind to fly
>   the speeders. As soon as each transport is
>   loaded, evacuation control will give clear-
>   ance for immediate launch.

>   REBEL FIGHTER
>   Right, sir.

INT. HOTH — REBEL BASE — MAIN HANGAR DECK

Alarms sound. Troops, ground crews, and droids rush to their alert
stations. Armored snowspeeders are lined up in attack formation near
the main entrance.

In the midst of all this activity, Han does some frantic welding on
the lifters of the Millennium Falcon.

Han finishes his work and hops down to the hangar floor. He pulls
out his comlink, all the while eyeing the problematic lifters.

>   HAN
>   (into comlink, to Chewie) Okay, that's it.
>   Try it . . . Off! Turn it off! Turn it
>   off! Off!!

Smoke rises from a minor explosion on the lifter. Exasperated, Han
surveys the new damage.

INT. REBEL BASE — MEDICAL CENTER

Luke dresses in readiness for the evacuation as his attending
medical droid stands by.

>   MEDICAL DROID
>   Sir, it will take quite a while to evacuate
>   the T-forty-sevens.

CONTINUED:

                         LUKE
          Well, forget the heavy equipment. There's
          plenty of time to get the smaller modules on
          the transports.

                         MEDICAL DROID
          Take care, sir.

                         LUKE
          Thanks.

INT. REBEL BASE — MAIN HANGAR DECK

Pilots, gunners, and R2 units scurry about. Luke, pulling on his
heavy-weather jacket, is headed toward a row of armored speeders. He
stops at the rear of the <u>Millennium Falcon</u>, where Han and Chewie are
trying to repair the right lifter with even more haste than before.

                         LUKE
          Chewie, take care of yourself, okay?

As Luke pats Chewie on the arm, Chewie puts his arms around Luke and
gives him a tight hug. Han is discussing the lifter with a repair
droid when he sees Luke.

                         HAN
          Hi, kid. (to droid) There's got to be a
          reason for it. Check it at the other end.
          Wait a second. (to Luke) You all right?

                         LUKE
          Yeah.

                         HAN
          Be careful.

                         LUKE
          You, too.

Luke smiles, then waves at his friend and walks on. After a few
steps, he stops and looks back. Han glances up and the two exchange
a silent communication, each wishing the other safety, happiness —
many things, all difficult to verbalize.

INT. REBEL BASE — CONTROL ROOM

Alarms sound throughout the hidden Rebel base. In the control room,
a controller urgently gestures for General Rieekan to check a
computer scan.

                         CONTROLLER
          General, there's a fleet of Star Destroyers
          coming out of hyperspace in sector four.

                                              (CONTINUED)

CONTINUED:

> RIEEKAN
>
> Reroute all power to the energy shield. We've
> got to hold them till all transports are
> away. Prepare for ground assault.

Rieekan exits hurriedly.

EXT. SPACE — IMPERIAL FLEET

Six huge Star Destroyers move through space into the Hoth system.

INT. VADER'S STAR DESTROYER — VADER'S CHAMBER —
MEDITATION CUBICLE

The dark cubicle is illuminated by a single shaft of light which
falls on the brooding Dark Lord as he sits on a raised meditation
cube. General Veers enters the room and approaches the silent,
unmoving Vader. Although seemingly very sure of himself, Veers is
still not bold enough to interrupt the meditating lord. The young
general stands quietly at attention until the evil presence speaks.

> VADER
>
> What is it, General?

> VEERS
>
> My lord, the fleet has moved out of light-
> speed. Com-Scan has detected an energy field
> protecting an area around the sixth planet of
> the Hoth system. The field is strong enough
> to deflect any bombardment.

> VADER
>
> (angrily) The Rebels are alerted to our
> presence. Admiral Ozzel came out of light-
> speed too close to the system.

> VEERS
>
> He felt surprise was wiser . . .

> VADER
>
> He is as clumsy as he is stupid. General,
> prepare your troops for a surface attack.

> VEERS
>
> Yes, my lord.

Veers turns smartly and leaves as Vader activates a large viewscreen
showing the bridge of his mighty ship. Admiral Ozzel appears on the
viewscreen, standing slightly in front of Captain Piett.

CONTINUED:

                          OZZEL
          Lord Vader, the fleet has moved out of light-
          speed, and we're preparing to . . . Aaagh!

                          VADER
          You have failed me for the last time,
          Admiral. Captain Piett.

Piett steps forward, as the admiral moves away, slightly confused,
touching his throat as it begins to constrict painfully.

                          PIETT
          Yes, my lord.

                          VADER
          Make ready to land our troops beyond the
          energy shield and deploy the fleet so that
          nothing gets off that system. You are in
          command now, Admiral Piett.

                          PIETT
          Thank you, Lord Vader.

Piett's pleasure about his unexpected promotion is not an unmixed
emotion. He glances warily at the struggling Admiral Ozzel who, with
a final choke, stumbles and falls in a lifeless heap before him.

INT. REBEL BASE — MAIN HANGAR DECK

With a sense of urgency, Leia quickly briefs a group of pilots
gathered in the center of the hangar.

                          LEIA
          All troop carriers will assemble at the
          north entrance. The heavy transport ships
          will leave as soon as they're loaded. Only
          two fighter escorts per ship. The energy
          shield can only be opened for a short time,
          so you'll have to stay very close to your
          transports.

                          HOBBIE
          Two fighters against a Star Destroyer?

                          LEIA
          The ion cannon will fire several shots to
          make sure that any enemy ships will be out of
          your flight path. When you've gotten past the
          energy shield, proceed directly to the
          rendezvous point. Understood?

                          PILOTS
          (in unison) Right. Okay.

                                              (CONTINUED)

CONTINUED:

                         LEIA
          Good luck.

                         DERLIN
          Okay. Everybody to your stations. Let's go!

The pilots hurry away.

EXT. HOTH — ICE PLAIN — SNOW TRENCH — DAY

Rebel troops carry heavy bazooka-type weapons and position them
along a snow trench. Men hurriedly respond to their officers' yelled
orders and brace themselves against the rhythmic gusts of bitter-
cold wind.

Other troops load power packs into a gun turret and swing its guns
into position.

EXT. HOTH — ICE PLAIN — POWER GENERATORS

Near the base power generators, troops rush to set up their heavy
battle equipment. Buzzing loudly, the generators send long, sparking
fingers of energy into the bitter Hoth wind.

INT. REBEL BASE — COMMAND CENTER

The long line of Rebel controllers is tense, as are Princess Leia
and General Rieekan, who are trying very hard not to show any fear.

                         RIEEKAN
          Their primary target will be the power genera-
          tors. Prepare to open shield.

EXT. ICE PLAIN

The Rebel transport and two escort fighters begin their departure
from the ice planet.

EXT. SPACE — IMPERIAL STAR DESTROYER

A huge Imperial Star Destroyer rests against a sea of stars, far
above the white surface of the planet Hoth.

INT. IMPERIAL STAR DESTROYER — BRIDGE

An Imperial controller approaches his commander.

                                                    (CONTINUED)

CONTINUED:

                              CONTROLLER
          Sir, Rebel ships are coming into our sector.

                               CAPTAIN
          Good. Our first catch of the day.

INT. REBEL BASE — COMMAND CENTER

                          WOMAN CONTROLLER
          Stand by, ion control . . . Fire!

EXT. REBEL BASE — ICE CAVE — ION CANNON

The giant ball-shaped ion cannon rotates into position and blasts
two red energy beams skyward.

EXT. SPACE — HOTH — REBEL TRANSPORT

The Rebel transport and its escorts race away from the white planet,
closely followed by the two red energy beams.

As the Rebel transport races toward the waiting Imperial Star
Destroyer, it is overtaken by the two scarlet energy bolts. The
Imperial Star Destroyer is hit in the conning tower by the powerful
bolts, which set up fiery explosions on its metal hull.

The big Destroyer veers, then spins wildly out of control. As the
Imperial ship careens into deep space, the Rebel transport races
away to safety.

INT. REBEL BASE — MAIN HANGAR DECK

Pilots, gunners, and troopers hurry to their stations and their
vehicles.

                              ANNOUNCER
                 (over loudspeaker) The first transport is
                 away.

Everyone cheers at the announcement, which echoes through the
hangar. Luke turns and walks on, heading toward his snowspeeder. His
gunner, Dack, a fresh-faced, eager kid, is glad to see him. They
climb in.

                                DACK
          Feeling all right, sir?

                                LUKE
          Just like new, Dack. How about you?

                                              (CONTINUED)

CONTINUED:

>   DACK
> Right now I feel like I could take on the
> whole Empire myself.
>
>   LUKE
> (quietly, strapping in) I know what you mean.

EXT. HOTH — ICE PLAIN

A thin horizon line cuts across the bleak landscape. Small dot-size objects begin to appear on the horizon, moving in the direction of the Rebel base.

EXT. HOTH — ICE PLAIN — SNOW TRENCH

A Rebel officer lifts a pair of electrobinoculars to his eyes. Through the lens he sees a very close view of a giant Imperial snow walker. He adjusts the view, which then zooms back to reveal three more of the ominous battle machines. Small flashes of yellow fire billow from the guns of the lumbering snow walkers.

The officer lowers his binoculars as the regular rhythmic pounding begins to make the ground vibrate. The pounding grows louder and is accompanied by a high-pitched, metallic rattling. The officer speaks into his comlink.

>   TRENCH OFFICER
> Echo Station Three-T-Eight.

INT. REBEL BASE — CORRIDOR

Pilots and gunners race to their waiting snowspeeders. Ice and snow begin falling from the walls of the corridor, shaken by the pounding Imperial snow walkers as they draw ever nearer.

>   TRENCH OFFICER
> (over comlink) We have spotted Imperial
> walkers!
>
>   CONTROLLER
> Imperial walkers on the north ridge.

EXT. HOTH — ICE PLAIN — SNOW TRENCH

The Rebel troops aim their weapons at the horizon as explosions erupt all around them. They are nervous and their grip on their weapons tightens from the cold and from fear.

Behind the troops a dozen snowspeeders race through the sky.

INT. LUKE'S SNOWSPEEDER, ROGUE LEADER — COCKPIT

                         LUKE
          (into comlink) Echo Station Five-seven. We're
          on our way.

EXT. HOTH — ICE PLAIN — BATTLEFIELD

The fleet of snowspeeders races above the ice field at full
throttle. They accelerate away from the base and head toward the
distant walkers.

INT. LUKE'S SNOWSPEEDER, ROGUE LEADER — COCKPIT

                         LUKE
          (into comlink) All right, boys, keep tight now.

                         DACK
          Luke, I have no approach vector. I'm not set.

                         LUKE
          Steady, Dack. Attack pattern delta. Go now!

EXT. HOTH — ICE PLAIN — BATTLEFIELD

The cannons mounted on a walker head fire at the speeders. Other
walkers loom in the background. Two speeders race away past two of
the enormous walkers and bank to the right.

INT. LUKE'S SNOWSPEEDER, ROGUE LEADER — COCKPIT

                         LUKE
              All right, I'm coming in.

He turns his speeder and heads directly at one of the walkers,
flying toward its towering legs. The horizon twists as the speeder
banks between the legs.

                         LUKE
          (into comlink) Hobbie, you still with me?

EXT. HOTH — ICE PLAIN — BATTLEFIELD

Two speeders race directly at the head of a walker, then split and
fly past it.

Three other walkers march onward, firing all cannons.

EXT. HOTH — ICE PLAIN — SNOW TRENCH

Rebel troops fire on the approaching walkers, as snow and ice
explode all around them.

EXT. HOTH — ICE PLAIN — BATTLEFIELD

A speeder banks through and away from the legs of a walker. Two
other speeders pass the first speeder from the opposite direction.
Others of the Rebel craft race just above the icy plain.

A giant walker head swivels and fires, striking a snowspeeder and
sending it crashing in a ball of flames.

INT. IMPERIAL SNOW WALKER — COCKPIT

General Veers and two walker pilots keep a careful eye on the racing
Rebel speeders as they maneuver their lumbering war machine forward.

Luke's speeder banks in from the side of Veers's walker and heads
straight for its viewport, blasting away. An explosion hits the
walker window, but dissipates, doing no harm. The speeder roars up
and over the impregnable war machine.

INT. LUKE'S SNOWSPEEDER, ROGUE LEADER — COCKPIT

Luke looks back at the walker as it grows smaller in the distance.

                    LUKE
          That armor's too strong for blasters.

On the horizon, another walker moves up past Luke's cockpit window,
twisting out of sight as Luke banks and starts another run.

                    LUKE
          (into comlink) Rogue Group, use your harpoons
          and tow cables. Go for the legs. It might be
          our only chance of stopping them. (to Dack)
          All right, stand by, Dack.

Dack is at the gunner's controls.

                    DACK
          Luke, we've got a malfunction in fire
          control. I'll have to cut in the auxiliary.

                    LUKE
          Just hang on. Hang on, Dack. Get ready to
          fire that tow cable.

                                              (CONTINUED)

CONTINUED:

Barely keeping his seat in the tumbling ship, Dack struggles to set up his harpoon gun.

Luke swings his speeder around and heads toward an oncoming walker. Laser bolts and flak fill the air, creating a deadly obstacle course for the tiny craft.

EXT. HOTH — ICE PLAIN — BATTLEFIELD

Rogue Leader and another snowspeeder fly in tight formation toward the walker as explosions burst all around them.

INT. LUKE'S SNOWSPEEDER, ROGUE LEADER — COCKPIT

After sustaining a heavy volley of fire, Luke turns around to see if Dack is all right.

                    LUKE
          Dack? Dack!

Dack is lost. Blood streams down his forehead, which rests on his smoldering controls. Out the back window, an Imperial walker recedes in the distance.

EXT. HOTH — ICE PLAIN — SNOW TRENCH AREA

Rebel troops fire the dishlike ray gun while explosions erupt around them.

EXT. HOTH — ICE PLAIN — BATTLEFIELD

Two walkers lumber toward the Rebel base as a speeder between them explodes in a ball of flames.

EXT. HOTH — ICE PLAIN — SNOW TRENCH

The dishlike ray gun is hit by a laser bolt and instantly explodes.

INT. IMPERIAL SNOW WALKER — COCKPIT

Through the cockpit window, Veers and his pilots can see the Rebel power generators in the distance.

A hologram of Darth Vader appears on a control panel screen.

(CONTINUED)

CONTINUED:

                         VEERS
          Yes, Lord Vader. I've reached the main power
          generators. The shield will be down in
          moments. You may start your landing.

INT. LUKE'S SNOWSPEEDER, ROGUE LEADER — COCKPIT

                         LUKE
               (into comlink) Rogue Three.

INT. WEDGE'S SNOWSPEEDER, ROGUE THREE — COCKPIT

                         WEDGE
               (into comlink) Copy, Rogue Leader.

                         LUKE
          (over comlink) Wedge, I've lost my gunner. You'll
          have to make this shot. I'll cover for you. Set
          your harpoon. Follow me on the next pass.

                         WEDGE
          (into comlink) Coming around, Rogue Leader.

INT. LUKE'S SNOWSPEEDER, ROGUE LEADER — COCKPIT

                         LUKE
               (into comlink) Steady, Rogue Two.

EXT. HOTH — BATTLEFIELD

Wedge's speeder races through the legs of one of the monstrous walkers.

INT. WEDGE'S SNOWSPEEDER, ROGUE THREE — COCKPIT

                         WEDGE
               (to gunner) Activate harpoon.

Wedge's gunner reaches for a firing switch to activate the harpoon.
The harpoon flashes out, and speeds toward the receding legs of the
walker.

EXT. HOTH — BATTLEFIELD

The harpoon hurtles toward the walker. In an instant it is embedded
in one of the walker's legs.

INT. WEDGE'S SNOWSPEEDER, ROGUE THREE — COCKPIT

                    WEDGE
          (to gunner) Good shot, Janson.

EXT. HOTH — BATTLEFIELD

The speeder Rogue Three races around one of the giant walker's feet,
trailing the cable behind it. Continuing around the back foot, Rogue
Three then circles the walker around the tail end.

INT. WEDGE'S SNOWSPEEDER, ROGUE THREE — COCKPIT

Wedge checks his controls and banks around the front of the walker.
                    WEDGE
          One more pass.
                    JANSON
          Coming around. Once more.

EXT. HOTH — BATTLEFIELD

The speeder sweeps left to right in front of the giant legs, towing
the cable behind it.

INT. WEDGE'S SNOWSPEEDER, ROGUE THREE — COCKPIT

                    JANSON
          Once more.
Wedge swings the speeder between the legs of the giant walker.
                    JANSON
          Cable out! Let her go!
                    WEDGE
          Detach cable.

EXT. WEDGE'S SNOWSPEEDER, ROGUE THREE

The cable release on the back of the speeder snaps loose and the
cable drops away.

INT. WEDGE'S SNOWSPEEDER, ROGUE THREE — COCKPIT

                    JANSON
        Cable detached.

EXT. HOTH — BATTLEFIELD

The speeder zooms away into the distance. The tangled legs of the
enormous war machine attempt a step, but as they do the giant
Imperial walker begins to topple. It teeters for a moment, and then
crashes onto the icy ground, sending snow and metal pieces flying.

EXT. HOTH — ICE PLAIN — SNOW TRENCH

The troops in the trenches cheer at the sight of the crashing
walker.

An officer gives a signal to his men and the Rebel troops charge the
fallen war machine.

                    TRENCH OFFICER
        Come on!

The troops run toward the downed walker, followed by two Rebel
speeders flying overhead. Just as they reach the walker, it
explodes, the impact throwing some of the men onto the frozen
ground.

INT. WEDGE'S SNOWSPEEDER, ROGUE THREE — COCKPIT

Wedge lets out a triumphant yell, banking his speeder away from the
fallen walker.

                    WEDGE
        (into comlink) Whooha!! That got him!

INT. LUKE'S SNOWSPEEDER, ROGUE LEADER — COCKPIT

                    LUKE
        (into comlink) I see it, Wedge. Good work.

INTEL BASE — COMMAND CENTER

Large chunks of ice tumble into the command center as Leia and
General Rieekan monitor computer screens.

                                              (CONTINUED)

CONTINUED:

> RIEEKAN
> I don't think we can protect two transports
> at a time.

> LEIA
> It's risky, but we can't hold out much
> longer. We have no choice.

> RIEEKAN
> (into comlink) Launch patrols.

> LEIA
> (to an aide) Evacuate remaining ground staff.

INT. REBEL BASE — MAIN HANGAR

Muffled distant explosions create widening cracks in the ice roof of
the hangar. Trying to ignore the noise and falling bits of snow, Han
works on one of the Falcon's lifters while Chewie works on one of
the wings. Noticing Chewie attach a wrong part, Han grows impatient.

> HAN
> No, no! No! This one goes there, that one
> goes there. Right?

In another area of the hangar, Threepio watches as Artoo is raised
up into Luke's X-wing fighter.

> THREEPIO
> Artoo, you take good care of Master Luke now,
> understand? And . . . do take good care of
> yourself. Oh, dear, oh, dear.

EXT. HOTH — BATTLEFIELD

The fierce battle on the vast snow plains of Hoth rages on. The
Imperial walkers continue their slow, steady assault on the Rebel
base, firing lasers as they lumber ever onward. In the snow trench,
Rebel troops fire large bazookalike guns and dishlike ray guns as
explosions erupt around them. A gun tower is hit by a laser bolt and
instantly explodes. Another blast destroys a ray gun.

INT. IMPERIAL SNOW WALKER — COCKPIT

General Veers studies various readouts on his control panel.

> VEERS
> All troops will debark for ground assault.
> Prepare to target the main generator.

EXT. HOTH — BATTLEFIELD

Luke's speeder and Rogue Two fly in formation, banking from right to
left and flying above the erupting battlefield. Flak bursts all
around them.

INT. LUKE'S SNOWSPEEDER, ROGUE LEADER — COCKPIT

Luke, glancing over, sees Rogue Two on his left. His ship shudders
as flak bursts nearby.

                         LUKE
             (into comlink) Rogue Two, are you all right?

INT. ZEV'S SNOWSPEEDER, ROGUE TWO — COCKPIT

                         ZEV
             (into comlink) Yeah. I'm with you, Rogue
             Leader.

INT. LUKE'S SNOWSPEEDER, ROGUE LEADER — COCKPIT

                         LUKE
             (into comlink) We'll set harpoon. I'll cover
             for you.

EXT. HOTH — BATTLEFIELD

The two speeders race across the horizon toward the giant walkers.

INT. ZEV'S SNOWSPEEDER, ROGUE TWO — COCKPIT

                         ZEV
             (into comlink) Coming around.

INT. LUKE'S SNOWSPEEDER, ROGUE LEADER — COCKPIT

                         LUKE
             (into comlink) Watch that crossfire, boys.

INT. ZEV'S SNOWSPEEDER, ROGUE TWO — COCKPIT

                    ZEV
          (into comlink) Set for position three. (to
          gunner) Steady.

                    LUKE
          (over comlink) Stay tight and low.

EXT. ZEV'S SNOWSPEEDER, ROGUE TWO

Luke's speeder moves in formation with Rogue Two, when suddenly
Zev's speeder is hit by a laser bolt. His ship bucks violently under
the impact and the cockpit explodes in a ball of flame.

Spewing smoke, the speeder hurtles toward a looming walker. Before
they collide, Rogue Two explodes in a million flaming pieces.

INT. LUKE'S SNOWSPEEDER, ROGUE LEADER — COCKPIT

Desperately, Luke works the controls of his flak-buffeted ship.
Suddenly, the speeder is rocked by a huge explosion. Luke struggles
with the controls with a look of terror on his face. The speeder
fills with smoke and electrical sparks jump about the cockpit.

                    LUKE
          (into comlink) Hobbie, I've been hit!

INT. REBEL BASE — COMMAND CENTER

Apart from the distant thunder of laser blasts, the corridor is
strangely quiet and empty. Running footsteps echo through the
freezing hallway, then Han appears. Cracks have appeared in some of
the walls and some pipes have broken, sending hot steam billowing
into the underground hallways. Han hurries into the command center.
It is a shambles, but some people are still at their posts. As he
enters, a gigantic cave-in almost obliterates the room. He finds
Leia and Threepio near one of the control boards.

                    HAN
          You all right?

Leia nods. She is surprised to see him.

                    LEIA
          Why are you still here?

                    HAN
          I heard the command center had been hit.

                                                    (CONTINUED)

CONTINUED:

                         LEIA
          You got your clearance to leave.

                         HAN
          Don't worry, I'll leave. First I'm going to
          get you to your ship.

                         THREEPIO
          Your Highness, we must take this last trans-
          port. It's our only hope.

                         LEIA
          (to controller) Send all troops in sector
          twelve to the south slope to protect the
          fighters.

A blast rocks the command center, throwing Threepio backward into
Han's arms.

                         ANNOUNCER
          (over loudspeaker) Imperial troops have
          entered the base.

                         HAN
          Come on . . . that's it.

                         LEIA
          (to head controller) Give the evacuation code
          signal. And get to your transports!

Leia looks exhausted. Han grabs her hand and starts to lead her out.

As Han, Leia, and Threepio run out of the command center, the code
signal can be heard echoing off the corridor walls.

                         HEAD CONTROLLER
          K-one-zero . . . all troops disengage.

                         THREEPIO
          (to Han and Leia) Oh! Wait for me!

EXT. BATTLEFIELD — SNOW TRENCH

Rebel troops retreat under the awesome Imperial onslaught.

                         OFFICER
          Begin retreat!

                         SECOND OFFICER
          Fall back!

Troops flee from the battle, the ground exploding around them.

EXT. HOTH — BATTLEFIELD

Three of the giant walkers, firing lasers, advance toward the Rebel headquarters.

EXT. HOTH — SNOW TRENCH

Continuing their retreat, the Rebels see the walkers looming ever nearer.

EXT. HOTH — BATTLEFIELD — ICE PLAIN

On the battlefield, Luke watches as a walker foot rises and moves over him. He looks up at the underbelly of the huge walker, passing overhead.

Running beneath the monstrous machine, Luke fires his harpoon gun at the walker's underside. A thin cable follows the projectile from the gun. The magnetic head and cable attach firmly to the metal hull.

Still running under the walker, Luke attaches the cable drum to his belt buckle. Soon he is pulled up the cable and hangs dangling underneath the walker.

The walker's giant feet continue to pound onward across the frozen snow. Stray laser bolts whistle by Luke as he climbs up the cable to the walker's hull, reaching a small hatch. Hanging precariously, Luke cuts the solid metal hatch with his laser sword.

He takes a land mine from around his neck and throws it inside the Imperial machine. Quickly, Luke starts down the cable and crashes onto the icy ground far below. He lies unconscious as a giant rear leg passes by — and just misses him.

The giant walker stops in midstep. A muffled explosion comes from within — and then the walker's mechanical insides are spewed out of every conceivable opening. The machine sits dead in its tracks, smoking like a locomotive on stilts.

EXT. HOTH — BATTLEFIELD

Veers's walker continues to advance toward the Rebel base. The smoldering walker that Luke exploded stands smoking just to the right of Veers's path.

INT. IMPERIAL SNOW WALKER — COCKPIT

Inside his walker, General Veers prepares to fire on the Rebel power
generators.

                    VEERS
          Distance to power generators?

                    PILOT
          One-seven, decimal two-eight.

Veers reaches for the electrorangefinder and lines up the main generator.

                    VEERS
          Target. Maximum fire power.

EXT. HOTH — BATTLEFIELD

The Rebel troops continue their desperate retreat, pushed back by
the relentless Imperial assault.

INT. HOTH — REBEL BASE — ICE CORRIDORS

With Threepio lagging behind, Han and Leia race through the
crumbling ice corridors. Suddenly, there is an explosion. Han turns,
grabs the princess, and pulls her to the wall as a tremendous cave-
in blocks their path.

He takes the comlink from his pocket.

                    HAN
          (into comlink) Transport, this is Solo.
          Better take off — I can't get to you. I'll
          get the princess out on the Falcon.

Han and Leia turn and race down the corridor.

                    THREEPIO
          But . . . but . . . but . . . where are you
          going? Uh . . . come back!!

INT. HOTH — REBEL BASE — COMMAND CENTER

Imperial troops have reached the base. As they push through the
blocked passageway, Darth Vader strides behind them.

INT. HOTH — REBEL BASE — ICE CORRIDOR

Han and Leia run toward the entrance of the main hangar where the
Millennium Falcon is docked. Threepio still lags behind.

                                        (CONTINUED)

CONTINUED:

                    THREEPIO
      Wait! Wait for me! Wait! Stop!

The door to the hangar closes in his face.

                    THREEPIO
      (exasperated) How typical.

Quickly, the door reopens as Han reaches out and pulls the golden
droid through.

                    HAN

      Come on.

INT. HOTH — REBEL BASE — MAIN HANGAR

Chewie paces under the shelter of the <u>Millennium Falcon</u>'s landing
gear. The giant Wookiee pats the underbelly of his beloved ship and
barks a few reassuring words. As he searches worriedly for his
captain, something at last catches his eye.

Chewie lets out a relieved shriek at seeing Han and Leia running
toward the ship. The Wookiee runs out into the falling ice, lets out
a howl, then runs up the ship's ramp. Han and Leia run up the ramp
after him, closely followed by Threepio.

                    HAN
      Hurry up, goldenrod, or you're going to be a
      permanent resident!

                    THREEPIO

      Wait! Wait!

INT. HOTH — REBEL BASE — ICE CORRIDOR

Imperial troops run through the base corridors. Vader surveys the
place. A huge ice chunk falls, almost hitting him, but he calmly,
purposefully, continues around it.

INT. REBEL BASE — MAIN HANGAR — MILLENNIUM FALCON

A distant, huge explosion rocks the hangar deck. Ice cakes come
crashing down on the <u>Millennium Falcon</u>.

INT. MAIN HANGAR — MILLENNIUM FALCON — MAIN HOLD

Han, standing before a control panel, is busy flipping switches as
Chewie watches a troublesome gauge. A worried Leia observes their
efforts.

                                                    (CONTINUED)

CONTINUED:

                    HAN
          (to Chewie) How's this?

The Wookiee barks a negative reply.

                    LEIA
          Would it help if I got out and pushed?

                    HAN
          It might.

Threepio clanks into the hold.

                    THREEPIO
          Captain Solo, Captain Solo . . . sir, might I
          suggest that you . . .

Han gives the gold robot a devastating look.

                    THREEPIO
          It can wait.

INT. MAIN HANGAR — MILLENNIUM FALCON — COCKPIT

They move to the cockpit where Han flips some more switches. Leia
watches him, impatient, disbelieving.

                    LEIA
          This bucket of bolts is never going to get us
          past that blockade.

                    HAN
          This baby's got a few surprises left in her,
          sweetheart.

Han and Leia look out the cockpit window and see a squad of
stormtroopers rushing into the far side of the hangar.

Quickly, Han straps himself into the pilot's seat and Leia gets into
the navigator's chair.

INT. HOTH — REBEL BASE — MAIN HANGAR

Stormtroopers hurriedly set up a large bazookalike weapon. Behind
them the giant hangar doors open slowly.

EXT. MAIN HANGAR — MILLENNIUM FALCON

A laser gun appears on the Falcon and swings around to aim at the
Imperial troops.

The stormtroopers, preparing to fire their bazooka cannon, are hit
by the Falcon's fire and are thrown about in all directions.

INT. MAIN HANGAR — MILLENNIUM FALCON — COCKPIT

Chewie rushes into the cockpit.

                    HAN
          Come on! Come on! Switch over. Let's hope we
          don't have a burnout.

A laser hits the window near Chewie as he is settling into his
chair. Letting out a loud whelp, Chewie quickly pulls back on the
controls and the first stage of engine fire can be heard. Han
flashes a big grin at Leia.

                    HAN
          See?

                    LEIA
          Someday you're going to be wrong, and I just
          hope I'm there to see it.

Han looks at Chewie.

                    HAN
          Punch it!

The roar of the Falcon's main engines blasts out everything as the
ice-cave wall rushes by outside the cockpit window.

INT. REBEL BASE — MAIN HANGAR

More stormtroopers run into the hangar, closely followed by Vader.
Hearing the loud roar of the Millennium Falcon's engines, Vader
looks toward the main hangar doors just in time to see the Falcon
lift up and disappear outside the cave.

EXT. HOTH — ICE SLOPE — DAY

Luke and two other pilots look up as the Millennium Falcon races
above them, flying very close to the ground.

The three pilots turn then, and trudge onward toward their X-wing
fighters, each going to his own ship. Luke waves farewell, then
heads toward his own fighter.

Artoo, seated in his cubbyhole, chirps an excited greeting as Luke
climbs aboard the spacecraft.

                    LUKE
          Artoo! Get her ready for takeoff.

From his ship, Luke sees Wedge in his own X-wing, preparing for
takeoff.

                                                   (CONTINUED)

CONTINUED:

                           WEDGE
          Good luck, Luke. See you at the rendezvous.

Luke smiles and nods at Wedge, then lowers himself into the cockpit
of his X-wing while Artoo waits in the cubbyhole, beeping
impatiently.

                           LUKE
          Don't worry, Artoo. We're going, we're going.

The canopy over the X-wing lowers and snaps shut.

EXT. SPACE — LUKE'S X-WING

Luke's fighter, its wings closed, speeds away from the icy planet.
Soon it disappears into the stars.

INT. LUKE'S X-WING — COCKPIT

Luke, looking thoughtful, suddenly makes a decision. He flips several
switches. The stars shift as he takes his fighter into a steep turn.
The X-wing banks sharply and flies away in a new direction.

The monitor screen on Luke's control panel prints out a question
from the concerned Artoo.

                           LUKE
          (into comlink) There's nothing wrong, Artoo.
          I'm just setting a new course.

Artoo beeps once again.

                           LUKE
          (into comlink) We're not going to regroup
          with the others.

Artoo begins a protest, whistling an unbelieving, "What?!"

Luke reads Artoo's exclamation on his control panel.

                           LUKE
          (into comlink) We're going to the Dagobah
          system.

Luke checks his readouts and makes a few adjustments. He rides along
with only the soft hum of the instruments to break the silence.
Finally, Artoo chirps up.

                           LUKE
          (into comlink) Yes, Artoo?

Artoo utters a soft, carefully phrased stream of whistles.

(CONTINUED)

CONTINUED:

                              LUKE
          (into comlink, chuckling) That's all right.
          I'd like to keep it on manual control for a
          while.

The little droid lets out a defeated whimper. Luke just smiles, and
continues on his course.

EXT. SPACE — MILLENNIUM FALCON

The Millennium Falcon speeds away from Hoth, closely followed by one
huge Star Destroyer and four tiny TIE fighters.

As it is pursued, the Falcon races toward two very bright star-size
objects.

INT. MILLENNIUM FALCON — COCKPIT

Inside the cockpit, Chewie lets out a loud howl. Han checks the
deflectors as the ship is buffeted by exploding flak. He appears to
be doing six things at once.

                              HAN
          (harried) I saw them! I saw them!

                              LEIA
          Saw what?

                              HAN
          Star Destroyers, two of them, coming right at us.

Threepio bumps and bangs his way into the cockpit.

                            THREEPIO
          Sir, sir! Might I suggest . . .

                              HAN
          (to Leia) Shut him up or shut him down! (to
          Chewie) Check the deflector shield!

Chewie barks a reply as he readjusts an overhead switch.

                              HAN
          Oh, great. Well, we can still outmaneuver them.

EXT. SPACE — MILLENNIUM FALCON — STAR DESTROYERS

The Millennium Falcon races toward one of the huge oncoming Star
Destroyers. Suddenly, the Falcon starts into a steep dive straight
down, closely followed by four TIE fighters. The underside of
the Star Destroyer continues on a collision course with the two
oncoming Star Destroyers. Slowly, it starts to veer to the left.

INT. STAR DESTROYER — BRIDGE

Out the front window, the two approaching Star Destroyers can be
seen veering to the left.

                    IMPERIAL OFFICER
          Take evasive action!

Alarms sound all over the huge ship. The two other Star Destroyers
get closer, one of them moving over the bridge so close that it
makes brushing contact with it.

EXT. SPACE — MILLENNIUM FALCON — TIE FIGHTERS

The Millennium Falcon races away from the colliding Star Destroyers,
still followed by four TIE fighters. Laser bolts spark the pitch-
black skies.

INT. MILLENNIUM FALCON — COCKPIT

Things have calmed down a bit, but the race isn't over yet. Chewie
barks at Han. Leia is still trying to recover from the steep dive.
The ship is buffeted by laser blasts.

                    HAN
          Prepare to make the jump to lightspeed.

                    THREEPIO
          But, sir!

The buffeting of the lasers becomes louder and stronger.

                    LEIA
          They're getting closer!

                    HAN
          (with a gleam in his eye) Oh, yeah?
          Watch this.

Expectantly, they look out the cockpit window as stars do not go
into hyperspace, but just sit there.

Han and Chewie look at each other and are thrown into an acute state
of concern.

                    LEIA
          Watch what?

Han tries again. Still nothing.

                    HAN
          I think we're in trouble.

                                              (CONTINUED)

CONTINUED:

                        THREEPIO
        If I may say so, sir, I noticed earlier the
        hyperdrive motivator has been damaged. It's
        impossible to go to lightspeed!

                        HAN
        We're in trouble!

The explosions become heavier.

EXT. SPACE — MILLENNIUM FALCON — TIE FIGHTERS — STAR DESTROYER

The Falcon races into the starry vastness, followed by the four
Imperial TIE fighters and an Imperial Star Destroyer.

INT. MILLENNIUM FALCON — COCKPIT

Stars race by as flak bursts outside the Falcon's window.

INT. MILLENNIUM FALCON — HOLD

Han works furiously at some control panels while giving various
orders to Chewie.

                        HAN
        Horizontal boosters . . . !

(Chewie barks)
        Alluvial dampers . . . ! Well, that's not it.

(Chewie barks)
        Bring me the hydrospanners!

Chewie hurries over to the pit and places the tools on the edge.

                        HAN
        I don't know how we're going to get out of
        this one.

Suddenly, a loud thump hits the side of the Falcon, causing it to lurch
radically. Chewie barks. The tools fall into the pit on top of Han.

                        HAN
        Oww! Chewie!

More turbulence rocks the ship.

                        HAN
        That was no laserblast! Something hit us.

                        LEIA
        (over comlink) Han, get up here!

                                                (CONTINUED)

CONTINUED:

                         HAN
          Come on, Chewie!

Han climbs out of the hold like a shot. Both he and Chewie run out
of the hold and toward the cockpit.

INT. MILLENNIUM FALCON — COCKPIT

Out the front cockpit window, they see hundreds of asteroids
racing by.

                         LEIA
          Asteroids!

Han changes places with Leia who has been at the controls, and
Chewie gets into his chair. Han works his controls as a chunk of
rock crosses in front of the ship.

                         HAN
          Oh, no! Chewie, set two-seven-one.

                         LEIA
          What are you doing? You're not actually going
          into an asteroid field?

                         HAN
          They'd be crazy to follow us, wouldn't they?

Another asteroid thumps against the ship and Leia winces at the jolt.

                         LEIA
          You don't have to do this to impress me.

                         THREEPIO
          Sir, the possibility of successfully navigat-
          ing an asteroid field is approximately three
          thousand seven hundred and twenty to one.

                         HAN
          Never tell me the odds!

EXT. ASTEROID BELT — MILLENNIUM FALCON

The Falcon turns into the asteroid storm and as the ship completes
its turn, asteroids start coming straight at the cockpit window.

A large asteroid tumbles away from the Falcon's path at top speed.
Several smaller asteroids crash into the big one, creating small
explosions on its surface. Other asteroids of all sizes pass by in
every direction, some colliding and exploding. The tiny Millennium
Falcon veers around the big asteroid and races past it through the
rain of rocks, followed by four TIE fighters, which bob and weave
around the asteroids.

                                              (CONTINUED)

CONTINUED:

One of the pursuing TIE fighters connects with an asteroid and explodes. The other fighters are pelted with a steady stream of smaller explosions.

Two huge asteroids tumble toward the <u>Millennium Falcon</u>, which quickly banks around both of them. The three TIE fighters follow in hot pursuit until one of the fighters scrapes an asteroid and tumbles out of control into deep space.

EXT. SPACE — STAR DESTROYER — ASTEROID BELT

The massive Star Destroyer blasts oncoming asteroids as it follows the <u>Falcon</u>. Smaller asteroids explode across its vast surface.

EXT. MILLENNIUM FALCON — TIE FIGHTERS — ASTEROID BELT

The <u>Falcon</u> twists on its side as it races around an oncoming asteroid. Two TIE fighters follow in the distance, coming from either side.

INT. MILLENNIUM FALCON — COCKPIT

Asteroids race by the cockpit window as Han pilots his trusty craft through the dangerous field.

Looking out the cockpit window, the <u>Falcon</u> crew sees a big asteroid drop past the window, narrowly missing their ship.

Chewie barks in terror as a slightly smaller asteroid comes especially close — too close — and bounces off the <u>Falcon</u> with a loud crunch. Threepio's hands cover his eyes. He manages a short peek at the cockpit window. Princess Leia sits stone-faced, staring at the action. Han gives her a quick look.

> HAN
> You said you wanted to be around when I made a mistake; well, this could be it, sweetheart.

> LEIA
> I take it back. We're going to get pulverized if we stay out here much longer.

The group watches as more asteroids race by outside the window.

> HAN
> I'm not going to argue with that.

> THREEPIO
> Pulverized?

(CONTINUED)

CONTINUED:

                         HAN
          I'm going in closer to one of those big ones.

                         LEIA
     Closer?

                         THREEPIO
     Closer?!

Chewbacca barks the same word, only louder.

EXT. MILLENNIUM FALCON — ASTEROID BELT

The Millennium Falcon dives toward the surface of one of the moon-
size asteroids. There is a continued display of explosions against
the starry void as smaller asteroids collide with larger chunks of
rock. The two remaining TIE fighters follow the Falcon to the large
asteroid. The Falcon skims the surface of the giant asteroid as, all
the while, small asteroids explode on the surface of the ship.

The TIE fighters approach the Falcon, but a giant asteroid hurtles
directly into their path. As the asteroid continues on its way, it
leaves the remains of the two exploded TIE fighters to tumble into
deep space.

INT. MILLENNIUM FALCON — COCKPIT

Rattled by the violent rocking of the starship, Threepio is nearly
in hysterics.

                         THREEPIO
          Oh, this is suicide!

Han notices something on his main scope and nudges his faithful
Wookiee, pointing.

                         HAN
          There. That looks pretty good.

                         LEIA
     What looks pretty good?

                         HAN
     Yeah. That'll do nicely.

                         THREEPIO
          (to Leia) Excuse me, ma'am, but where are we
          going?

Out the cockpit window, they see that they are skimming the surface
of the enormous asteroid and nearing a large crater.

EXT. MILLENNIUM FALCON — GIANT ASTEROID CRATER

The Millennium Falcon dives into the huge crater and disappears.

INT. MILLENNIUM FALCON — COCKPIT

                         LEIA
          I hope you know what you're doing.

                         HAN
          Yeah, me, too.

INT. GIANT ASTEROID CRATER

The Falcon races down into the crater. The walls are barely visible
as the ship speeds through the tunnel-like opening. A small cave
appears on one side of the crater, and the Falcon turns, slows, and
scoots into it.

EXT. SPACE — LUKE'S X-WING

The tiny X-wing speeds toward the cloud cover of Dagobah. Artoo,
riding on the back of the fighter, turns his head back and forth
with some anxiety.

INT. LUKE'S X-WING — COCKPIT

Luke watches Artoo's words as they are translated and screened on
the computer scope.

                         LUKE
          (into comlink) Yes, that's it. Dagobah.

Artoo beeps a hopeful inquiry.

                         LUKE
          (into comlink) No, I'm not going to change my
          mind about this. (getting a little nervous)
          I'm not picking up any cities or technology.
          Massive life-form readings, though. There's
          something alive down there . . .

Again, Artoo beeps, this time a slightly worried question.

                         LUKE
          (into comlink) Yes, I'm sure it's perfectly
          safe for droids.

EXT. SPACE — DAGOBAH — LUKE'S X-WING

The X-wing continues its flight through the twilight above the cloud-covered planet.

INT. LUKE'S X-WING — COCKPIT

Luke sees the clouds race by as he takes his craft closer to the planet. He must operate his controls carefully since the cloud cover has completely obscured his vision. An alarm buzzes in the background. Artoo beeps and whistles frantically.

                    LUKE
          (into comlink) I know, I know! All the scopes
          are dead. I can't see a thing! Just hang on,
          I'm going to start the landing cycle . . .

The blast of the retrorockets is deafening, drowning out Artoo's electronic squeals. Suddenly, there is a cracking sound as if limbs were being broken off trees and then a tremendous jolt as the space-craft stops. Luke pulls a switch and his canopy pops open.

EXT. DAGOBAH — DUSK

The mist-shrouded X-wing fighter is almost invisible in the thick fog. Luke climbs out onto the long nose of the spacecraft as Artoo pops out of his cubbyhole on the back. The young warrior surveys the fog, which is barely pierced by the ship's landing lights. About all he can make out are some giant, twisted trees nearby. Artoo whistles anxiously.

                    LUKE
          No, Artoo, you stay put. I'll have a look
          around.

Artoo lets out a short beep. As Luke moves along the nose, Artoo loses his balance and disappears with a splash into the boggy lake.

                    LUKE
          Artoo?

Luke kneels and leans over the plane looking for Artoo, but the water is still and reveals no sign of the little droid.

                    LUKE
          Artoo! Where are you?

A small periscope breaks the surface of the water and a gurgly beep is heard. The periscope starts to move to shore. Relieved, Luke starts running along the nose of the fighter to its tip.

                                        (CONTINUED)

CONTINUED:

                              LUKE
              Artoo! You be more careful.

The outline of the shore is now no more than ten feet away. Luke
jumps off the plane into the water, scrambles up to the shore, and
turns to look for Artoo. The periscope still steadily moves toward
shore.

                              LUKE
              Artoo — that way!

Suddenly, through the thick fog layer, a dark shape appears, moving
toward the little droid. The dark, sinuous bog beast dives beneath
the swampy water, making a loud clunk against Artoo's metal hull.
The droid disappears from sight, uttering a pathetic electronic
scream.

Holding his ignited lightsaber before him, Luke wades a few feet
into the murky pool, looking for any sign of his little friend.

                              LUKE
              Artoo!

The black surface is still as death itself . . . until a few bubbles
begin to appear. Then, <u>phheewaat</u>!! The runt-size robot is spit out
of the water, makes a graceful arc, and comes crashing down into a
patch of soft gray moss.

                              LUKE
              Oh, no! Are you all right? Come on. You're
              lucky you don't taste very good. Anything
              broken?

Luke helps Artoo to his feet and begins wiping the mud and roots
from his round metal body. Artoo responds with feeble, soggy beeps.

                              LUKE
              If you're saying coming here was a bad idea,
              I'm beginning to agree with you. Oh, Artoo,
              what are we doing here? It's like . . . some-
              thing out of a dream, or, I don't know. Maybe
              I'm just going crazy.

As Luke glances around at the spooky swamp jungle that surrounds
him, Artoo ejects a stream of muddy water from one of his cranial
ports.

EXT. VADER'S STAR DESTROYER — VADER'S CHAMBER

Admiral Piett hesitates in the entryway to Vader's private cubicle.
After a moment, he steps into the room and pauses at the surprising
sight before him.

                                                      (CONTINUED)

[51]

CONTINUED:

Darth Vader, his back turned, is silhouetted in the gloom on the far
side of the chamber. A black, insectlike droid attends him. Among
the various apparatuses surrounding them, a respirator tube now
retracts from Vader's uncovered head. The head is bald with a mass
of ugly scar tissue covering it. The black droid then lowers the
mask and helmet onto Vader's head. When it is in place, the Dark
Lord turns to face Piett.

                    VADER
          Yes, Admiral?

                    PIETT
          Our ships have sighted the Millennium Falcon,
          Lord. But . . . it has entered an asteroid
          field and we cannot risk . . .

                    VADER
          (interrupting) Asteroids do not concern me,
          Admiral. I want that ship and not excuses.

                    PIETT
          Yes, Lord.

EXT. ASTEROID CAVE — MILLENNIUM FALCON

The pirate starship rests in a dark, dripping asteroid cave. It
is so dark that the cave's exact dimensions are impossible to
determine.

INT. MILLENNIUM FALCON — COCKPIT

Han and Chewie busily shut down the engine and all electronic
systems. Threepio and Leia watch worriedly.

                    HAN
          I'm going to shut down everything but the
          emergency power systems.

                    THREEPIO
          Sir, I'm almost afraid to ask, but . . . does
          that include shutting me down, too?

Chewie barks "Yes." But Han thinks otherwise.

                    HAN
          No, I need you to talk to the Falcon, find
          out what's wrong with the hyperdrive.

Suddenly, the ship lurches, causing all the loose items in the
cockpit to go flying. Chewie howls.

                                            (CONTINUED)

CONTINUED:

> THREEPIO
> Sir, it's quite possible this asteroid is not
> entirely stable.

> HAN
> Not entirely stable? I'm glad you're here to
> tell us these things. Chewie, take the profes-
> sor in the back and plug him into the hyper-
> drive.

> THREEPIO
> Oh! Sometimes I just don't understand human
> behavior. After all, I'm only trying to do my
> job in the most . . .

The sliding door closes behind the indignant Threepio as Chewie and
he move back to the hold. Suddenly, the ship lurches again, throwing
Leia across the cabin into Han's arms. Then, abruptly, the motion
stops as suddenly as it started. With some surprise, Han and Leia
realize they are in each other's arms.

> LEIA
> Let go.

> HAN
> Sshh!

> LEIA
> Let go, please.

Leia flushes, averting her eyes. She's not exactly fighting to get
free. But, of course, Han blows it . . .

> HAN
> Don't get excited.

The anger rises in Leia.

> LEIA
> Captain, being held by you isn't quite enough
> to get me excited.

> HAN
> Sorry, sweetheart. We haven't got time for
> anything else.

Han grins wickedly at Leia as he turns and exits through the door.
Leia's confused emotions show clearly on her lovely face.

EXT. DAGOBAH — BOG CLEARING — DUSK

The mist has dispersed a bit, but it is still a very gloomy-looking
swamp.

(CONTINUED)

CONTINUED:

Luke pulls an equipment box from the shore to the clearing. He ignites a little fusion furnace and warms his hands before it. Taking a power cable, he plugs it into Artoo's noselike socket.

                    LUKE
          Ready for some power? Okay. Let's see now.
          Put that in there. There you go.

The droid whistles his appreciation. Luke then opens a container of processed food and sits before the thermal heater.

                    LUKE
          (sighs) Now all I have to do is find this
          Yoda . . . if he even exists.

Nervously, he looks around at the foreboding jungle.

                    LUKE
          It's really a strange place to find a Jedi
          Master. It gives me the creeps.

Artoo beeps in agreement with that sentiment.

                    LUKE
          Still . . . there's something familiar about
          this place. I feel like . . . I don't know . . .

                    STRANGE VOICE
          Feel like what?

Luke jumps out of his skin. Artoo screeches in terror. The young warrior grabs for his lightsaber as he spins around, looking for the speaker. Mysteriously standing right in front of Luke is a strange, bluish creature, not more than two feet tall. The wizened little thing is dressed in rags. It motions toward Luke's sword.

                    LUKE
          (looking at the creature) Like we're being
          watched!

                    CREATURE
          Away put your weapon! I mean you no harm.

After some hesitation, Luke puts away his weapon, although he really doesn't understand why. Artoo watches with interest.

                    CREATURE
          I am wondering, why are you here?

                    LUKE
          I'm looking for someone.

                    CREATURE
          Looking? Found someone, you have, I would
          say, hmmm?

The little creature laughs.

                                        (CONTINUED)

CONTINUED:

                                 LUKE
(trying to keep from smiling) Right.

                            CREATURE
Help you I can. Yes, mmmm.

                                 LUKE
I don't think so. I'm looking for a great
warrior.

                            CREATURE
Ahhh! A great warrior. (laughs and shakes his
head) Wars not make one great.

With the aid of a walking stick, the tiny stranger moves over to one
of the cases of supplies. He begins to rummage around.

Artoo moves to the edge of the case — standing almost eye level to
the creature who is carelessly handling the supplies — and squeaks
his disapproval.

Their tiny visitor picks up the container of food Luke was eating
from and takes a bite.

                                 LUKE
Put that down. Hey! That's my dinner!

The creature spits out the bite he has taken. He makes a face.

                            CREATURE
How you get so big, eating food of this kind?

He flips the container in Luke's direction and reaches into one of
Luke's supply cases.

                                 LUKE
Listen, friend, we didn't mean to land in that
puddle, and if we could get our ship out, we
would, but we can't, so why don't you just . . .

                            CREATURE
(teasing) Aww, cannot get your ship out?

The creature starts rummaging through Luke's case, throwing the
contents out behind him.

                                 LUKE
Hey, get out of there!

                            CREATURE
Ahhh! No!

The creature spots something of interest in Luke's case. Luke loses
patience and grabs the case away. The creature retains his prize — a
tiny power lamp — and examines it with delight.

(CONTINUED)

CONTINUED:

                        LUKE
        Hey, you could have broken this. Don't do
        that. Ohhh . . . you're making a mess. Hey,
        give me that!

                        CREATURE
        (retreating with the lamp) Mine! Or I will
        help you not.

Clutching its treasure, the creature backs away from Luke, drawing
closer to Artoo. As Luke and the creature argue, one of Artoo's
little arms slowly moves out toward the power lamp, completely
unnoticed by the creature.

                        LUKE
        I don't want your help. I want my lamp back.
        I'll need it to get out of this slimy
        mudhole.

                        CREATURE
        Mudhole? Slimy? My home this is.

Artoo grabs hold of the lamp and the two little figures are immediately engaged in a tug-of-war over it.

Artoo beeps a few angry, "Give me thats."

                        CREATURE
        Ah, ah, ah!

                        LUKE
        Oh, Artoo, let him have it.

                        CREATURE
        Mine! Mine!

                        LUKE
        Artoo!

                        CREATURE
        Mine!

The creature lets go with one hand and pokes Artoo lightly with one
finger. Artoo reacts with a startled squeal, and lets go.

                        CREATURE
        Mine!

                        LUKE
        (fed up) Now will you move along, little
        fella? We've got a lot of work to do.

                        CREATURE
        No! No, no! Stay and help you, I will.
        (laughs) Find your friend, hmm?

                                        (CONTINUED)

CONTINUED:

                        LUKE
          I'm not looking for a friend, I'm looking for
          a Jedi Master.

                        CREATURE
          Oohhh. Jedi Master. Yoda. You seek Yoda.

                        LUKE
          You know him?

                        CREATURE
          Mmm. Take you to him, I will. (laughs) Yes,
          yes. But now, we must eat. Come. Good food.
          Come.

With that, the creature scurries out of the clearing, laughing
merrily. Luke stares after him. All he sees is the faint light from
the small power lamp moving through the fog. Luke makes his decision
and starts after the creature.

                        CREATURE
          (in the distance) Come, come.

Artoo, very upset, whistles a blue streak of protests.

                        LUKE
          Stay here and watch after the camp, Artoo.

Artoo beeps even more frantically. But as Luke disappears from
view, the worried little droid grows quieter, and utters a soft
electronic sigh.

INT. MILLENNIUM FALCON — MAIN HOLD AREA

Threepio whistles and beeps a strange dialect into the control panel
in front of him. The control panel whistles back a few mystifying
beeps.

                        THREEPIO
          Oh, where is Artoo when I need him?

Han enters the hold area and kneels on the floor near the control box.

                        THREEPIO
          Sir, I don't know where your ship learned to
          communicate, but it has the most peculiar
          dialect. I believe, sir, it says that the
          power coupling on the negative axis has
          been polarized. I'm afraid you'll have to
          replace it.

                        HAN
          Well, of course I'll have to replace it.

Han Solo searches for Luke Skywalker who was ambushed on the icy Hoth snow plains and narrowly escaped becoming a meal for a wampa.

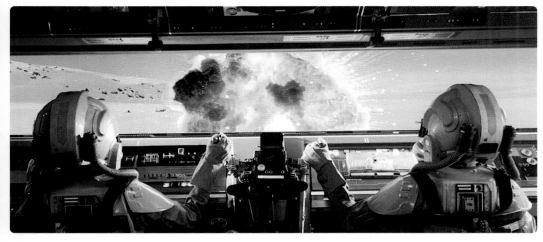

Only the valiant efforts by the Rebel forces enabled the Rebels to escape the Imperial assault, spearheaded by the massive and deadly AT-AT walkers.

Luke Skywalker played a pivotal role in the Rebel delaying action.

Darth Vader himself led the attack on the Rebel stronghold. He was backed up by Imperial snowtroopers.

Luke journeyed to Dagobah,
where the Jedi Master
Yoda instructed him in the
ways of the Force.

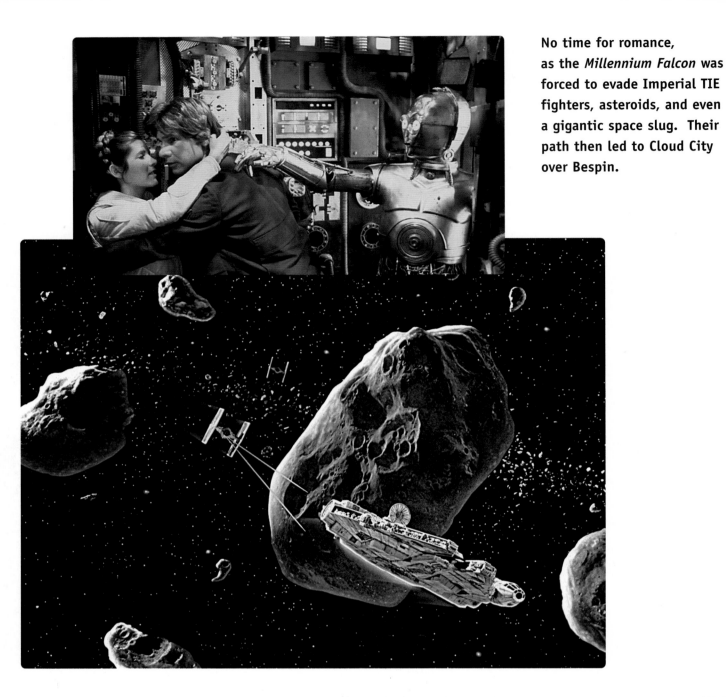

No time for romance, as the *Millennium Falcon* was forced to evade Imperial TIE fighters, asteroids, and even a gigantic space slug. Their path then led to Cloud City over Bespin.

Landing at Cloud City, the fugitives were greeted by an old "friend," Lando Calrissian, who showed them the wonders of his floating metropolis.

Cornered, Lando was
forced to collaborate
with Darth Vader, who
had hired Boba Fett to
track the *Falcon*.

Vader set a trap for Luke Skywalker,
and tested his containment method
on Han Solo, freezing him in carbonite.

In the midst of a duel with Vader, Luke lost a hand, and learned that Vader was his father.

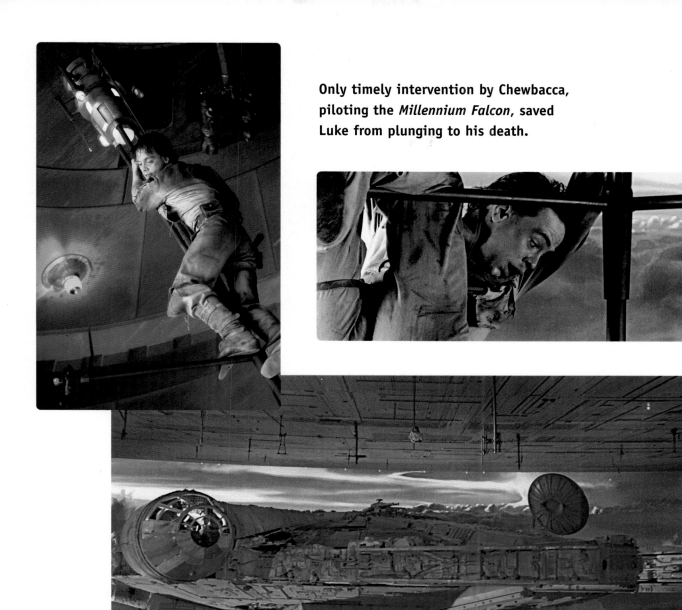

Only timely intervention by Chewbacca,
piloting the *Millennium Falcon*, saved
Luke from plunging to his death.

A battered Rebel fleet
sought a safe haven and
a place to heal.

Luke, Leia, and the droids said their farewells as Lando and
Chewie began the search for Han.

CONTINUED:

He hands a wire coil up to Chewie who is working near the ceiling.

                    HAN
          Here! And, Chewie . . .

Chewie brings his head back through the trap door in the ceiling and
whines. Han glances back at Threepio, then speaks quietly to Chewie
so only he can hear.

                    HAN
          (continued) . . . I think we'd better replace
          the negative power coupling.

Leia finishes welding the valve she has been working on and attempts
to reengage the system by pulling a lever attached to the valve. It
doesn't budge. Han notices her struggle, and moves to help her. She
rebuffs him.

                    HAN
          Hey, Your Worship, I'm only trying to help.

                    LEIA
          (still struggling) Would you please stop
          calling me that?

Han hears a new tone in her voice. He watches her pull on the lever.

                    HAN
          Sure, Leia.

                    LEIA
          Oh, you make it so difficult sometimes.

                    HAN
          I do, I really do. You could be a little nicer,
          though. (he watches her reaction) Come on,
          admit it. Sometimes you think I'm all right.

She lets go of the lever and rubs her sore hand.

                    LEIA
          Occasionally (a little smile, haltingly)
          maybe . . . when you aren't acting like a
          scoundrel.

                    HAN
          (laughs) Scoundrel? Scoundrel? I like the
          sound of that.

With that, Han takes her hand and starts to massage it.

                    LEIA
          Stop that.

                    HAN
          Stop what?

Leia is flushed, confused.

                              (CONTINUED)

CONTINUED:

                              LEIA
          Stop that! My hands are dirty.

                              HAN
          My hands are dirty, too. What are you
          afraid of?

                              LEIA
          (looking right into his eyes) Afraid?

Han looks at her with a piercing look. He's never looked more
handsome, more dashing, more confident. He reaches out slowly and
takes Leia's hand again from where it is resting on a console. He
draws it toward him.

                              HAN
          You're trembling.

                              LEIA
          I'm not trembling.

Then with an irresistible combination of physical strength and
emotional power, the space pirate begins to draw Leia toward
him . . . very slowly.

                              HAN
          You like me because I'm a scoundrel. There
          aren't enough scoundrels in your life.

Leia is now very close to Han and as she speaks, her voice becomes
an excited whisper, a tone completely in opposition to her words.

                              LEIA
          I happen to like nice men.

                              HAN
          I'm a nice man.

                              LEIA
          No, you're not. You're . . .

He kisses her now, with slow, hot lips. He takes his time, as though
he had forever, bending her body backward. She has never been kissed
like this before, and it almost makes her faint. When he stops, she
regains her breath and tries to work up some indignation, but finds
it hard to talk.

Suddenly, Threepio appears in the doorway, speaking excitedly.

                              THREEPIO
          Sir, sir! I've isolated the reverse power
          flux coupling.

Han turns slowly, icily, from their embrace.

                              HAN
          Thank you. Thank you very much.

                                                    (CONTINUED)

CONTINUED:

                        THREEPIO
         Oh, you're perfectly welcome, sir.

The moment spoiled, Han marches out after Threepio.

EXT. SPACE — ASTEROID FIELD

The Imperial fleet moves through the asteroid-filled void, intently
seeking its prey.

INT. VADER'S STAR DESTROYER — BRIDGE

Asteroids collide, creating a fireworks display outside the bridge
window. Darth Vader stands, staring out the window above the control
deck. Then he slowly turns toward the bridge. Before him are the
hologram images of twenty battleship commanders. One of these
images, the commander of a ship that has just exploded, is fading
quickly away. Another image, in the center and a little apart from
the others, is faded and continually disrupted by static. It is the
image of Captain Needa, commander of the Star Destroyer most hotly
on the tail of the Millennium Falcon. Admiral Piett and an aide
stand behind the Dark Lord.

                        NEEDA
         (in hologram) . . . and that, Lord Vader, was
         the last time they appeared in any of our
         scopes. Considering the amount of damage we've
         sustained, they must have been destroyed.

                        VADER
         No, Captain, they're alive. I want every ship
         available to sweep the asteroid field until
         they are found.

The Imperial star captains fade out one by one as Vader turns to
Admiral Piett.

                        PIETT
         Lord Vader.

                        VADER
         Yes, Admiral, what is it?

The admiral is scared, his face white as a sheet.

                        PIETT
         The Emperor commands you to make contact
         with him.

                        VADER
         Move the ship out of the asteroid field so
         that we can send a clear transmission.

                                              (CONTINUED)

CONTINUED:

                              PIETT
          Yes, my lord.

EXT. ASTEROID FIELD — VADER'S STAR DESTROYER

Vader's Imperial Star Destroyer moves against the vast sea of stars
away from the rest of the fleet.

INT. VADER'S STAR DESTROYER — VADER'S CHAMBER

The Dark Lord, Darth Vader, is alone in his chamber. A strange sound
enters the room and light begins to play across Vader's black
figure. He looks up and bows quickly.

A twelve-foot hologram of the Galactic Emperor materializes before
Vader. The Emperor's dark robes and monk's hood are reminiscent of
the cloak worn by Ben Kenobi. His voice is even deeper and more
frightening than Vader's.

                              VADER
          What is thy bidding, my master?

                              EMPEROR
          There is a great disturbance in the Force.

                              VADER
          I have felt it.

                              EMPEROR
          We have a new enemy — Luke Skywalker.

                              VADER
          Yes, my master.

                              EMPEROR
          He could destroy us.

                              VADER
          He's just a boy. Obi-Wan can no longer
          help him.

                              EMPEROR
          The Force is strong with him. The son of
          Skywalker must not become a Jedi.

                              VADER
          If he could be turned, he would become a
          powerful ally.

                              EMPEROR
          Yes. Yes. He would be a great asset. Can it
          be done?

                                              (CONTINUED)

CONTINUED:

                    VADER
        He will join us or die, my master.

Vader kneels. The supreme Emperor passes a hand over the crouched
Lord of the Sith and fades away.

EXT. DAGOBAH — CREATURE'S HOUSE — NIGHT

A heavy downpour of rain pounds through the gnarled trees. A strange
baroque mud house sits on a moss-covered knoll on the edge of a
small lagoon. The small, gnomish structure radiates a warm glow from
its thick glass windows. As the rain tap-dances a merry tune on
Artoo's head, the stubby little droid rises up on his tip-toes to
peek into one of the glowing portals.

INT. CREATURE'S HOUSE

Artoo, peeking in the window, sees the inside of the house — a very
plain, but cozy dwelling. Everything is in the same scale as the
creature. The only thing out of place in the miniature room is Luke,
whose height makes the four-foot ceiling seem even lower. He sits
cross-legged on the floor of the living room.

The creature is in an adjoining area — his little kitchen — cooking
up an incredible meal. The stove is a steaming hodgepodge of pots
and pans. The wizened little host scurries about chopping this,
shredding that, and showering everything with exotic herbs and
spices. He rushes back and forth putting platters on the table in
front of Luke, who watches the creature impatiently.

                    LUKE
        Look, I'm sure it's delicious. I just don't
        understand why we can't see Yoda now.

                    CREATURE
        Patience! For the Jedi it is time to eat as
        well. Eat, eat. Hot. Good food, hm? Good, hmm?

Moving with some difficulty in the cramped quarters, Luke sits down
near the fire and serves himself from the pot. Tasting the unfamil-
iar concoction, he is pleasantly surprised.

                    LUKE
        How far away is Yoda? Will it take us long to
        get there?

                    CREATURE
        Not far. Yoda not far. Patience. Soon you
        will be with him. (tasting food from the
        pot) Rootleaf, I cook. Why wish you become
        Jedi? Hm?

                                                    (CONTINUED)

CONTINUED:

>   LUKE
> Mostly because of my father, I guess.

>   CREATURE
> Ah, your father. Powerful Jedi was he,
> powerful Jedi, mmm.

>   LUKE
> (a little angry) Oh, come on. How could you
> know my father? You don't even know who I am.
> (fed up) Oh, I don't know what I'm doing
> here. We're wasting our time.

The creature turns away from Luke and speaks to a third party.

>   CREATURE
> (irritated) I cannot teach him. The boy has
> no patience.

Luke's head spins in the direction the creature faces. But there is
no one there. The boy is bewildered, but it gradually dawns on him
that the little creature is Yoda, the Jedi Master, and that he is
speaking with Ben.

>   BEN'S VOICE
> He will learn patience.

>   YODA
> Hmmm. Much anger in him, like his father.

>   BEN'S VOICE
> Was I any different when you taught me?

>   YODA
> Hah. He is not ready.

>   LUKE
> Yoda! I am ready. I . . . Ben! I can be a
> Jedi. Ben, tell him I'm ready.

Trying to see Ben, Luke starts to get up but hits his head on the
low ceiling.

>   YODA
> Ready, are you? What know you of ready? For
> eight hundred years have I trained Jedi. My own
> counsel will I keep on who is to be trained! A
> Jedi must have the deepest commitment, the most
> serious mind. (to the invisible Ben, indicating
> Luke) This one a long time have I watched. All
> his life has he looked away . . . to the
> future, to the horizon. Never his mind on where
> he was. Hmm? What he was doing. Hmph. Adventure.
> Heh! Excitement. Heh! A Jedi craves not these
> things. (turning to Luke) You are reckless!

(CONTINUED)

CONTINUED:

Luke looks down. He knows it is true.

                    BEN'S VOICE
          So was I, if you'll remember.

                    YODA
          He is too old. Yes, too old to begin the
          training.

Luke thinks he detects a subtle softening in Yoda's voice.

                    LUKE
          But I've learned so much.

Yoda turns his piercing gaze on Luke, as though the Jedi Master's
huge eyes could somehow determine how much the boy has learned.
After a long moment, the little Jedi turns toward where he alone
sees Ben.

                    YODA
          (sighs) Will he finish what he begins?

                    LUKE
          I won't fail you — I'm not afraid.

                    YODA
          (turns slowly toward him) Oh, you will be.
          You will be.

EXT. SPACE — STAR DESTROYERS — ASTEROID FIELD

The Imperial fleet around Vader's ship is surrounded by the asteroid
storm. Asteroids big and small pelt the vast exteriors of the
menacing ships. One of the smaller Imperial vessels is hit by a huge
asteroid and explodes in a brilliant flash of light.

INT. ASTEROID CAVE — MILLENNIUM FALCON — COCKPIT

The cockpit is quiet and lit only by the indicator lights on the
control panel. Princess Leia sits in the pilot's seat. She runs her
hand across the control panel as she thinks of Han and the confusion
he has created within her. Suddenly, something outside the cockpit
window catches her eye. The reflection of the panel lights obscures
her vision until a soft suctionlike cup attaches itself to the
windscreen. Leia moves closer to see what it might be. Large, yellow
eyes flash open and stare back at her. Startled, she jumps back into
her seat, her heart pounding. There is a scurry of feet and a loud
screech, and in an instant the eyes are gone. The young princess
catches her breath, jumps out of her chair, and races from the
cockpit.

INT. ASTEROID CAVE — MILLENNIUM FALCON — HOLD AREA

The lights go bright for a second, then go out again. Threepio and Chewbacca watch as Han finishes with some wires.

                         THREEPIO
              Sir, if I may venture an opinion . . .

                         HAN
              I'm not really interested in your opinion,
              Threepio.

Leia rushes into the cabin just as Han drops the final floor panel into place.

                         LEIA
              (out of breath) There's something out
              there.

                         HAN
              Where?

                         LEIA
              Outside, in the cave.

As she speaks, there comes a sharp banging on the hull. Chewie looks up and barks anxiously.

                         THREEPIO
              There it is. Listen! Listen!

                         HAN
              I'm going out there.

                         LEIA
              Are you crazy?!

                         HAN
              I just got this bucket back together. I'm not
              going to let something tear it apart.

He and Chewie grab their breath masks off a rack and hurry out. Leia follows.

                         LEIA
              Then I'm going with you.

                         THREEPIO
              I think it might be better if I stay behind
              and guard the ship. (hears another mysterious
              noise) Oh, no.

EXT. ASTEROID CAVE — MILLENNIUM FALCON

It is very dark and dank inside the huge asteroid cave, too dark to see what is attacking the ship.

                                              (CONTINUED)

CONTINUED:

Leia stamps her foot on the floor of the cave.

                    LEIA
          This ground sure feels strange. It doesn't
          feel like rock at all.

Han kneels and studies the ground, then attempts to study the
outline of the cave.

                    HAN
          There's an awful lot of moisture in here.

                    LEIA
          I don't know. I have a bad feeling about this.

                    HAN
     Yeah.

Chewie barks through his face mask, and points toward the ship's
cockpit. A five-foot-long shape can be seen moving across the top of
the Falcon. The leathery creature lets out a screech as Han blasts
it with a laserbolt.

                    HAN
          (to Leia) Watch out!

The black shape tumbles off the spaceship and onto the ground in front
of the princess. Han bends down to investigate the dead creature.

                    HAN
          Yeah, that's what I thought. Mynock. Chewie,
          check the rest of the ship, make sure there
          aren't any more attached. They're chewing on
          the power cables.

                    LEIA
     Mynocks?

                    HAN
          Go on inside. We'll clean them off if there
          are any more.

Just then, a swarm of the ugly creatures swoops through the air.
Leia puts her arms over her head to protect herself as she runs
toward the ship. Chewie shoos another mynock away with his blaster.
Several of the batlike creatures flap their wings loudly against the
cockpit window of the Falcon. Inside, Threepio shudders at their
presence.

                    THREEPIO
          Ohhh! Go away! Go away! Beastly thing. Shoo!
          Shoo!

Han looks around the strange, dripping cave.

                    HAN
          Wait a minute . . .

CONTINUED:

He unholsters his blaster and fires at the far side of the huge
cave. The cavern begins to shake and the ground starts to buckle.

Chewie barks and moves for the ship, followed closely by Leia and
Han. The large wings of the mynocks flap past them as they protect
their faces and run up the platform.

INT. ASTEROID CAVE — MILLENNIUM FALCON — ENTRY AREA

As soon as Han and Leia are on board, Chewie closes the main hatch.
The ship continues to shake and heave.

                    HAN
          All right, Chewie, let's get out of here!

The Wookiee heads for the cockpit as Han, followed by Threepio,
rushes to the hold area and checks the scopes on the control panel.
Leia hurries after.

                    LEIA
          The Empire is still out there. I don't think
          it's wise to . . .

Han rushes past her and heads for the cockpit.

                    HAN
          (interrupting) No time to discuss this in
          committee.

And with that he is gone. The main engines of the Falcon begin to
whine. Leia races after him, bouncing around in the shaking ship.

                    LEIA
          (angry) I am not a committee!

INT. ASTEROID CAVE — MILLENNIUM FALCON — COCKPIT

Han is already in the pilot's seat pulling back on the throttle. The
cave-quake has greatly diminished.

                    LEIA
          You can't make the jump to lightspeed in this
          asteroid field . . .

                    HAN
          Sit down, sweetheart. We're taking off!

As the ship begins to move forward, Chewie barks. He notices
something out the window ahead. Threepio sees it, too.

                    THREEPIO
          Look!

                                        (CONTINUED)

CONTINUED:

                              HAN
          I see it, I see it.

Suddenly, a row of jagged white stalagmites and stalactites can be
seen surrounding the entrance. And as the Falcon moves forward, the
entrance to the cave grows ever smaller. Han pulls hard on the
throttle, sending his ship surging forward.

                            THREEPIO
          We're doomed!

                              LEIA
          The cave is collapsing.

                              HAN
          This is no cave.

                              LEIA
          What?

Leia's mouth drops open. She sees that the rocks of the cave
entrance are not rocks at all, but giant teeth, quickly closing
around the tiny ship. Chewie howls.

INT. SPACE SLUG MOUTH

The Millennium Falcon, zooming through the monster's mouth, rolls on
its side and barely makes it between two of the gigantic white teeth
before the huge jaw slams closed.

EXT. CAVE ENTRANCE — GIANT ASTEROID

The enormous space slug moves its head out of the cave as the Falcon
flies out of its mouth. The monster tilts its head, watching the
starship fly away.

EXT. MILLENNIUM FALCON — GIANT ASTEROID

The Falcon races out of the asteroid crater and into the deadly rain
of the asteroid storm.

EXT. DAGOBAH — DAY

With Yoda strapped to his back, Luke climbs up one of the many thick
vines that grow in the swamp. Panting heavily, he continues his
course — climbing, flipping through the air, jumping over roots, and
racing in and out of the heavy ground fog.

                                                         (CONTINUED)

CONTINUED:

                         YODA
          Run! Yes. A Jedi's strength flows from the
          Force. But beware of the dark side. Anger
          . . . fear . . . aggression. The dark side of
          the Force are they. Easily they flow, quick
          to join you in a fight. If once you start
          down the dark path, forever will it dominate
          your destiny, consume you it will, as it did
          Obi-Wan's apprentice.

                         LUKE
          Vader. Is the dark side stronger?

                         YODA
          No . . . no . . . no. Quicker, easier, more
          seductive.

                         LUKE
          But how am I to know the good side from the
          bad?

                         YODA
          You will know. When you are calm, at peace.
          Passive. A Jedi uses the Force for knowledge
          and defense, never for attack.

                         LUKE
          But tell me why I can't . . .

                         YODA
          (interrupting) No, no, there is no why.
          Nothing more will I teach you today. Clear
          your mind of questions. Mmm. Mmmmmm.

Artoo beeps in the distance as Luke lets Yoda down to the ground.
Breathing heavily, he takes his shirt from a nearby tree branch and
pulls it on.

He turns to see a huge, dead, black tree, its base surrounded by a
few feet of water. Giant, twisted roots form a dark and sinister
cave on one side. Luke stares at the tree, trembling.

                         LUKE
          There's something not right here.

Yoda sits on a large root, poking his gimer stick into the dirt.

                         LUKE
          I feel cold, death.

                         YODA
          That place . . . is strong with the dark side
          of the Force. A domain of evil it is. In you
          must go.

                                                    (CONTINUED)

CONTINUED:

                              LUKE
          What's in there?

                              YODA
          Only what you take with you.

Luke looks warily between the tree and Yoda. He starts to strap on
his weapon belt.

                              YODA
          Your weapons . . . you will not need them.

Luke gives the tree a long look, then shakes his head "no." Yoda
shrugs. Luke reaches up to brush aside some hanging vines and enters
the tree.

INT. DAGOBAH — TREE CAVE

Luke moves into the almost total darkness of the wet and slimy cave.
The youth can barely make out the edge of the passage.

Holding his lit saber before him, he sees a lizard crawling up the
side of the cave and a snake wrapped around the branches of a tree.
Luke draws a deep breath, then pushes deeper into the cave.

The space widens around him, but he feels that rather than sees it.
His sword casts the only light as he peers into the darkness. It is
very quiet here.

Then, a loud hiss! Darth Vader appears across the blackness, illuminated by his own just-ignited laser sword. Immediately, he charges
Luke, saber held high. He is upon the youth in seconds, but Luke
sidesteps perfectly and slashes at Vader with his sword.

Vader is decapitated. His helmet-encased head flies from his shoulders as his body disappears into the darkness. The metallic banging
of the helmet fills the cave as Vader's head spins and bounces,
smashes on the floor, and finally stops. For an instant it rests on
the floor, then it cracks vertically. The black helmet and breath
mask fall away to reveal . . . Luke's head.

Across the space, the standing Luke gasps at the sight, wide-eyed in
terror.

The decapitated head fades away, as in a vision.

EXT. DAGOBAH — CAVE — DUSK

Meanwhile, Yoda sits on the root, calmly leaning on his gimer stick.

EXT. SPACE — VADER'S STAR DESTROYER

Vader's Imperial Star Destroyer moves through space, guarded by its convoy of TIE fighters.

INT. VADER'S STAR DESTROYER — BRIDGE — CONTROL DECK

Vader stands in the back control area of his ship's bridge with a motley group of men and creatures. Admiral Piett and two controllers stand at the front of the bridge and watch the group with scorn.

                         PIETT
          Bounty hunters. We don't need that scum.

                    FIRST CONTROLLER
          Yes, sir.

                         PIETT
          Those Rebels won't escape us.

A second controller interrupts.

                    SECOND CONTROLLER
          Sir, we have a priority signal from the Star
          Destroyer Avenger.

                         PIETT
          Right.

The group standing before Vader is a bizarre array of galactic fortune hunters: There is Bossk, a slimy, tentacled monster with two huge, bloodshot eyes in a soft baggy face; Zuckuss and Dengar, two battle-scarred, mangy human types; IG-88, a battered, tarnished chrome war droid; and Boba Fett, a man in a weapon-covered armored space suit.

                         VADER
          . . . there will be a substantial reward for
          the one who finds the Millennium Falcon. You
          are free to use any methods necessary, but I
          want them alive. No disintegrations.

                       BOBA FETT
          As you wish.

At that moment, Admiral Piett approaches Vader in a rush of excitement.

                         PIETT
          Lord Vader! My lord, we have them.

EXT. IMPERIAL STAR DESTROYER, AVENGER — ASTEROID BELT

The Millennium Falcon speeds through deep space, closely followed by a firing Imperial Star Destroyer. A large asteroid about the same size as the Falcon tumbles rapidly toward the starship. The tiny Falcon banks to avoid the giant asteroid as smaller rocks pelt its surface. Then the small craft roars under the asteroid, which explodes harmlessly on the hull of the vast Star Destroyer.

INT. MILLENNIUM FALCON — COCKPIT

The ship shudders as flak explodes near the cockpit window. Threepio checks a tracking scope on the side control panel while Leia watches tensely out the window.

                    THREEPIO
          Oh, thank goodness we're coming out of the
          asteroid field.

Chewie barks excitedly as the rain of asteroids begins to subside. A bolt from the Star Destroyer sets up a fiery explosion on the back side of the Falcon, causing it to lurch to one side.

EXT. MILLENNIUM FALCON — STAR DESTROYER, AVENGER — ASTEROID FIELD

The Falcon is hit hard by another bolt from the Star Destroyer, which creates a huge explosion near the cockpit of the smaller ship. The Falcon tilts steeply, then rights itself.

INT. MILLENNIUM FALCON — COCKPIT

Han corrects the angle of his ship.

                    HAN
          Let's get out of here. Ready for lightspeed?
          One . . . two . . . three!

Han pulls back on the hyperspace throttle and — nothing happens. Flak bursts continue to rock the ship.

                    HAN
          (frantic) It's not fair!

Chewie is very angry and starts to growl and bark at his friend and captain. Again, Han desperately pulls back on the throttle.

                    HAN
          The transfer circuits are working. It's not
          my fault!

                                        (CONTINUED)

CONTINUED:

Chewie puts his head in his hands, whining.

LEIA
(almost expecting it) No lightspeed?

HAN
It's not my fault.

THREEPIO
Sir, we just lost the main rear deflector shield. One more direct hit on the back quarter and we're done for.

Han pauses for a moment, makes a decision, and pulls back on a lever.

HAN
Turn her around.

Chewie barks in puzzlement.

HAN
I said turn her around! I'm going to put all power in the front shield.

LEIA
You're going to attack them?!

THREEPIO
Sir, the odds of surviving a direct assault on an Imperial Star Destroyer . . .

LEIA
Shut up!

EXT. SPACE — MILLENNIUM FALCON — ASTEROID FIELD

The Falcon banks, making a steep, twisting turn. In the next moment it is racing toward the Star Destroyer, looking very small against the massive surface of the Imperial ship. As it moves across the surface of the Star Destroyer, the Falcon bobs and weaves to avoid the numerous flak bursts.

INT. STAR DESTROYER, AVENGER — BRIDGE

The tiny Falcon heads directly for the Avenger's bridge. The Imperials stationed there are stunned to see the small spaceship racing low across the hull, headed directly at the huge windows of the bridge area. Alarms go off everywhere. The Destroyer's commander, Captain Needa, can scarcely believe his eyes.

NEEDA
They're moving to attack position. Shields up!

(CONTINUED)

CONTINUED:

Needa and his men duck as the <u>Falcon</u> nears the bridge window. At the last minute, the <u>Falcon</u> veers off and out of sight. All is quiet.

> NEEDA
> Track them. They may come around for another
> pass.

> TRACKING OFFICER
> Captain Needa, the ship no longer appears on
> our scopes.

> NEEDA
> They can't have disappeared. No ship that
> small has a cloaking device.

> TRACKING OFFICER
> Well, there's no trace of them, sir.

> COMMUNICATIONS OFFICER
> Captain, Lord Vader demands an update on the
> pursuit.

> NEEDA
> (drawing a breath) Get a shuttle ready. I
> shall assume full responsibility for losing
> them, and apologize to Lord Vader. Meanwhile,
> continue to scan the area.

> COMMUNICATIONS OFFICER
> Yes, Captain Needa.

EXT. DAGOBAH — BOG — DAY

Luke's face is upside-down and showing enormous strain. He stands on his hands, with Yoda perched on his feet. Opposite Luke and Yoda are two rocks the size of bowling balls. Luke stares at the rocks and concentrates. One of the rocks lifts from the ground and floats up to rest on the other.

> YODA
> Use the Force. Yes . . .

Yoda taps Luke's leg. Quickly, Luke lifts one hand from the ground. His body wavers, but he maintains his balance. Artoo, standing nearby, is whistling and beeping frantically.

> YODA
> Now . . . the stone. Feel it.

Luke concentrates on trying to lift the top rock. It rises a few feet, shaking under the strain. But, distracted by Artoo's frantic beeping, Luke loses his balance and finally collapses. Yoda jumps clear.

(CONTINUED)

CONTINUED:

                          YODA
              Concentrate!

Annoyed at the disturbance, Luke looks over at Artoo, who is rocking
urgently back and forth in front of him.

Artoo waddles closer to Luke, chirping wildly, then scoots over to
the edge of the swamp. Catching on, Luke rushes to the water's edge.
The X-wing fighter has sunk, and only the tip of its nose shows
above the lake's surface.

                          LUKE
              Oh, no. We'll never get it out now.

Yoda stamps his foot in irritation.

                          YODA
              So certain are you. Always with you it cannot
              be done. Hear you nothing that I say?

Luke looks uncertainly out at the ship.

                          LUKE
              Master, moving stones around is one thing.
              This is totally different.

                          YODA
              No! No different! Only different in your
              mind. You must unlearn what you have learned.

                          LUKE
              (focusing, quietly) All right, I'll give it a try.

                          YODA
              No! Try not. Do. Or do not. There is no try.

Luke closes his eyes and concentrates on thinking the ship out.

Slowly, the X-wing's nose begins to rise above the water. It hovers
for a moment and then slides back, disappearing once again.

                          LUKE
              (panting heavily) I can't. It's too big.

                          YODA
              Size matters not. Look at me. Judge me by my
              size, do you? Hm? Mmmm.

Luke shakes his head.

(CONTINUED)

CONTINUED:

                         YODA
        And well you should not. For my ally is the
        Force. And a powerful ally it is. Life creates
        it, makes it grow. Its energy surrounds us and
        binds us. Luminous beings are we . . . (Yoda
        pinches Luke's shoulder) . . . not this crude
        matter. (a sweeping gesture) You must feel
        the Force around you. (gesturing) Here,
        between you . . . me . . . the tree . . . the
        rock . . . everywhere! Yes, even between this
        land and that ship!

                         LUKE
        (discouraged) You want the impossible.

Quietly, Yoda turns toward the sunken X-wing fighter. With his eyes
closed and his head bowed, he raises his arm and points at the ship.

Soon, the fighter rises above the water and moves forward as Artoo
beeps in terror and scoots away.

The entire X-wing moves majestically, surely, toward the shore. Yoda
stands on a tree root and guides the fighter carefully down toward
the beach.

Luke stares in astonishment as the fighter settles gently onto the
shore. He walks toward Yoda.

                         LUKE
        I don't . . . I don't believe it.

                         YODA
        That is why you fail.

Luke shakes his head, bewildered.

EXT. SPACE — IMPERIAL FLEET

The fleet around Vader's Star Destroyer now includes Needa's Star
Destroyer, the Avenger.

INT. VADER'S STAR DESTROYER — BRIDGE

                         VADER
        Apology accepted, Captain Needa.

Clutching desperately at his throat, Captain Needa slumps down,
then falls over on his back, at the feet of Darth Vader. Two
stormtroopers pick up the lifeless body and carry it quickly away as
Admiral Piett and two of his captains hurry up to the Dark Lord.

(CONTINUED)

CONTINUED:

                              PIETT
          Lord Vader, our ships have completed their
          scan of the area and found nothing. If the
          Millennium Falcon went into lightspeed, it'll
          be on the other side of the galaxy by now.

                              VADER
          Alert all commands. Calculate every possible
          destination along their last known trajectory.

                              PIETT
          Yes, my lord. We'll find them.

                              VADER
          Don't fail me again, Admiral.

Vader exits as the admiral turns to an aide, a little more uneasy
than when he arrived.

                              PIETT
          Alert all commands. Deploy the fleet.

EXT. SPACE — IMPERIAL FLEET

Vader's ship moves away, flanked by its fleet of smaller ships. The
Avenger glides off into space in the opposite direction. No one on
that ship or on Vader's is aware that, clinging to the side of the
Avenger, is the pirateship, the Millennium Falcon.

INT. MILLENNIUM FALCON — COCKPIT

                              THREEPIO
          Captain Solo, this time you have gone too
          far. (Chewie growls) No, I will not be quiet,
          Chewbacca. Why doesn't anyone listen to me?

                              HAN
          (to Chewie) The fleet is beginning to break
          up. Go back and stand by the manual release
          for the landing claw.

Chewie barks, struggles from his seat, and climbs out of the cabin.

                              THREEPIO
          I really don't see how that is going to help.
          Surrender is a perfectly acceptable alterna-
          tive in extreme circumstances. The Empire may
          be gracious enough . . .

Leia reaches over and shuts off Threepio, midsentence.

                                                      (CONTINUED)

CONTINUED:

                         HAN
        Thank you.

                         LEIA
        What did you have in mind for your next move?

                         HAN
        Well, if they follow standard Imperial proce-
        dure, they'll dump their garbage before they
        go to lightspeed, then we just float away.

                         LEIA
        With the rest of the garbage. Then what?

                         HAN
        Then we've got to find a safe port somewhere
        around here. Got any ideas?

                         LEIA
        No. Where are we?

                         HAN
        The Anoat system.

                         LEIA
        Anoat system. There's not much there.

                         HAN
        No. Well, wait. This is interesting. Lando.

He points to a computer mapscreen on the control panel. Leia slips
out of her chair and moves next to the handsome pilot. Small light
points representing several systems flash by on the computer screen.

                         LEIA
        Lando system?

                         HAN
        Lando's not a system, he's a man. Lando
        Calrissian. He's a card player, gambler,
        scoundrel. You'd like him.

                         LEIA
        Thanks.

                         HAN
        Bespin. It's pretty far, but I think we can
        make it.

                         LEIA
        (reading from the computer) A mining colony?

                         HAN
        Yeah, a Tibanna gas mine. Lando conned
        somebody out of it. We go back a long way,
        Lando and me.

(CONTINUED)

CONTINUED:

                              LEIA
          Can you trust him?

                              HAN
          No. But he has no love for the Empire, I can
          tell you that.

Chewie barks over the intercom. Han quickly changes his readouts and
stretches to look out the cockpit window.

                              HAN
          (into intercom) Here we go, Chewie. Stand by.
          Detach!

Han leans back in his chair and gives Leia an inviting smile. She
thinks for a moment, shakes her head; a grin creeps across her face
and she gives him a quick kiss.

                              LEIA
          You do have your moments. Not many, but you
          have them.

EXT. SPACE — IMPERIAL STAR DESTROYER

As the Avenger Star Destroyer moves slowly into space, the hatch on
its underbelly opens, sending a trail of junk floating behind it.
Hidden among the refuse, the Falcon tumbles away. In the next
moment, the Avenger roars off into hyperspace. The Falcon's engines
are ignited, and it races off into the distance. Amid the slowly
drifting junk, Boba Fett's ship appears and moves after the Falcon.

EXT. DAGOBAH — BOG — CLEARING — DAY

In the clearing behind Yoda's house, Luke again stands upside-down,
but his face shows less strain and more concentration than before.
Yoda sits on the ground below the young warrior. On the other side
of the clearing, two equipment cases slowly rise into the air.
Nearby Artoo watches, humming to himself, when suddenly he, too,
rises into the air. His little legs kick desperately and his head
turns frantically, looking for help.

                              YODA
          Concentrate . . . feel the Force flow. Yes.
          Good. Calm, yes. Through the Force, things
          you will see. Other places. The future . . .
          the past. Old friends long gone.

Luke suddenly becomes distressed.

                              LUKE
          Han! Leia!

                                                    (CONTINUED)

CONTINUED:

The two packing boxes and Artoo fall to the ground with a crash,
then Luke himself tumbles over.

                    YODA
          (shaking his head) Hmm. Control, control. You
          must learn control.

                    LUKE
          I saw . . . I saw a city in the clouds.

                    YODA
          Mmm. Friends you have there.

                    LUKE
          They were in pain.

                    YODA
          It is the future you see.

                    LUKE
          Future? Will they die?

Yoda closes his eyes and lowers his head.

                    YODA
          Difficult to see. Always in motion is the
          future.

                    LUKE
          I've got to go to them.

                    YODA
          Decide you must how to serve them best. If
          you leave now, help them you could. But you
          would destroy all for which they have fought
          and suffered.

Luke is stopped cold by Yoda's words. Gloom shrouds him as he nods
his head sadly.

EXT. BESPIN SYSTEM — MILLENNIUM FALCON — DAWN

The powerful pirate starship blasts through space as it heads toward
the soft pink planet of Bespin.

EXT. BESPIN SURFACE — MILLENNIUM FALCON

It is dawn on the gaseous planet. Huge billowing clouds form a
canyon as the ship banks around them, headed toward the system's
Cloud City.

Suddenly, two twin-pod cloud cars appear and move toward the Falcon.
The cloud cars draw up alongside the starship.

INT. MILLENNIUM FALCON — COCKPIT

One of the cloud cars opens fire on the Falcon, its flak rocking the
ship. Chewie barks his concern.

                    HAN
          (into transmitter) No, I don't have a landing
          permit. I'm trying to reach Lando Calrissian.

More flak bursts outside the cockpit window and rattles the ship's
interior. Leia looks worried.

                    HAN
          (into transmitter) Whoa! Wait a minute! Let
          me explain.

                    INTERCOM VOICE
          You will not deviate from your present course.

                    THREEPIO
          Rather touchy, aren't they?

                    LEIA
          I thought you knew this person.

Chewie barks and growls at his boss.

                    HAN
          (to Chewie) Well, that was a long time ago.
          I'm sure he's forgotten about that.

                    INTERCOM VOICE
          Permission granted to land on Platform Three-
          two-seven.

                    HAN
          (into transmitter) Thank you.

Angry, Han snaps off the intercom. Chewie looks at him and grunts.
Han turns to the worried princess and her droid.

                    HAN
          There's nothing to worry about. We go way
          back, Lando and me.

Leia doesn't look convinced.

                    LEIA
          Who's worried?

EXT. CLOUD CITY — MILLENNIUM FALCON — CLOUD CARS

The clouds part to reveal a full view of the city as it bobs in and   ←Replace
out of the cloud surface. The cloud cars and the Falcon head for the   with insert
gleaming white metropolis.   from page
                                                                        80A for
                                                                        the
                                                                        Special
                                                                        Edition

SPECIAL EDITION INSERT TO PAGE 80

The clouds part to reveal a full view of the city as it bobs in and out of the cloud surface. The cloud cars and the <u>Falcon</u> head for the gleaming white metropolis. As the <u>Falcon</u> and the cloud cars approach the city, they bank around a large structure and fly in toward the landing platform.

EXT. CLOUD CITY — LANDING PLATFORM — MILLENNIUM FALCON

With the cloud cars still guarding it, the <u>Falcon</u> lands on one of the Cloud City's platforms.

EXT. LANDING PLATFORM — DOOR OF MILLENNIUM FALCON

Han and Leia stand at the open door, armed. Behind them, Chewie, also armed, surveys the scene warily.

                    THREEPIO
          Oh. No one to meet us.

                    LEIA
          I don't like this.

                    HAN
          Well, what would you like?

                    THREEPIO
          Well, they <u>did</u> let us land.

                    HAN
          Look, don't worry. Everything's going to be
          fine. Trust me.

INT. CLOUD CITY — CORRIDOR — DAY

Lando Calrissian, a suave, dashing black man in his thirties, leads a group of aides and some Cloud City guards rapidly toward the landing platform. The group, like the other citizens of the city, is a motley collection of aliens, droids, and humans of all descriptions. Lando has a grim expression on his face as he moves onto the landing platform.

EXT. LANDING PLATFORM — DOOR OF MILLENNIUM FALCON

                    HAN
          See? My friend. (to Chewie) Keep your eyes
          open, okay?

Chewie growls as Han walks down the ramp. Lando and his men head across the bridge to meet the space pirate.

EXT. CLOUD CITY — LANDING PLATFORM

Lando stops ten feet from Han. The two men eye each other carefully. Lando shakes his head.

                                        (CONTINUED)

CONTINUED:

                    LANDO
        Why, you slimy, double-crossing, no-good
        swindler! You've got a lot of guts coming
        here, after what you pulled.

Han points to himself innocently, mouthing, "Me?"

Lando moves threateningly toward Han. Suddenly, he throws his arms
around his startled, long-lost friend and embraces him.

                    LANDO
        (laughs) How you doing, you old pirate? So
        good to see you! I never thought I'd catch up
        with you again. Where you been?

The two old friends embrace, laughing and chuckling.

EXT. LANDING PLATFORM — DOOR OF MILLENNIUM FALCON

                    THREEPIO
        Well, he seems very friendly.

                    LEIA
        (wary) Yes . . . very friendly.

EXT. CLOUD CITY — LANDING PLATFORM

                    LANDO
        What are you doing here?

                    HAN
        (gestures toward the Falcon) Ahh . . .
        repairs. I thought you could help me out.

                    LANDO
        (in mock panic) What have you done to my ship?

                    HAN
        Your ship? Hey, remember, you lost her to me
        fair and square.

Chewie, Leia, and Threepio have made their way down the ramp.

                    LANDO
        And how are you doing, Chewbacca? You still
        hanging around with this loser?

Chewie growls a reserved greeting. Lando suddenly notices the
princess and smiles admiringly.

(CONTINUED)

CONTINUED:

                         LANDO
          Hello. What have we here? Welcome. I'm Lando
          Calrissian. I'm the administrator of this
          facility. And who might you be?

                         LEIA
          Leia.

                         LANDO
          Welcome, Leia.

Lando bows before Leia and kisses her hand.

                         HAN
          All right, all right, you old smoothie.

Han takes Leia by the hand and steers her away from Lando.

                         THREEPIO
          Hello, sir. I am See-Threepio, human-cyborg
          relations. My facilities are at your . . .

Before Threepio can finish his self-introduction, Lando has turned
to follow Han and Leia, who are walking toward the city.

                         THREEPIO
          Well, really!

Lando, his aide, Lobot, and Han lead the way across the bridge,
followed by Threepio, Chewie, and Leia.

                         LANDO
          What's wrong with the Falcon?

                         HAN
          Hyperdrive.

                         LANDO
          I'll get my people to work on it.

                         HAN
          Good.

Lando turns to Leia.

                         LANDO
          You know, that ship saved my life quite a few
          times. She's the fastest hunk of junk in the
          galaxy.

INT. CLOUD CITY — CORRIDOR

The group has crossed the narrow bridge and entered the city. They
walk down the lovely Art Deco passageway, rounding several corners
and passing many small plazas as they go. Threepio lags a bit
behind.

                                                    (CONTINUED)

CONTINUED:

                    HAN
        How's the gas mine? Is it still paying off
        for you?

                    LANDO
        Oh, not as well as I'd like. We're a small
        outpost and not very self-sufficient. And
        I've had supply problems of every kind. I've
        had labor difficulties . . . (catches Han
        grinning at him) What's so funny?

                    HAN
        You. Listen to you — you sound like a
        businessman, a responsible leader. Who'd have
        thought that, huh?

Lando is reflective. He looks at Han a moment.

                    LANDO
        You know, seeing you sure brings back a few
        things.

                    HAN
        Yeah.

                    LANDO
        (shakes his head) Yeah, I'm responsible these
        days. It's the price you pay for being
        successful.

Han and Lando laugh together, and the group moves on through the
corridor.

The lagging Threepio passes a Threepio-type silver droid who is
coming out of a door.

                    THREEPIO
        Oh! Nice to see a familiar face.

                    SECOND THREEPIO
        (mumbles) E chu ta!

                    THREEPIO
        How rude!

Threepio stops, watching the silver droid move away. Then he hears the
muffled beeping and whistling of an R2 unit coming from within the room.

INT. CLOUD CITY — ANTEROOM

Curious, Threepio enters the room.

                    THREEPIO
        That sounds like an R2 unit in there. I
        wonder if . . .

                                        (CONTINUED)

CONTINUED:

Threepio walks through the doorway to the main room. He looks in.

                    THREEPIO
          Hello? How interesting. Oh, my.

                    MAN'S VOICE
          (from within) Who are you?

                    THREEPIO
          Oh, I'm terrible sorry. I . . . I didn't mean
          to intrude. No, no, please don't get up. No!

A laser bolt to Threepio's chest sends him flying in twenty directions. Smoldering mechanical arms and legs bounce off the walls as
the door whooshes closed behind him.

INT. CLOUD CITY — CORRIDOR

Lando, Han, and Leia continue down the corridor unaware of
Threepio's dreadful accident. Chewbacca glances around, sniffs the
air, but shrugs his shoulders and follows the group.

EXT. DAGOBAH — BOG — DUSK

In the bright lights of the fighter, Luke loads a heavy case into
the belly of the ship. Artoo sits on top of the X-wing, settling
down into his cubbyhole. Yoda stands nearby on a log.

                    YODA
          Luke! You must complete the training.

                    LUKE
          I can't keep the vision out of my head.
          They're my friends. I've got to help them.

                    YODA
          You must not go!

                    LUKE
          But Han and Leia will die if I don't.

                    BEN'S VOICE
          You don't know that.

Luke looks toward the voice in amazement. Ben has materialized as a
real, slightly shimmering image near Yoda. The power of his presence
stops Luke.

                    BEN
          Even Yoda cannot see their fate.

                    LUKE
          But I can help them! I feel the Force!

                                        (CONTINUED)

CONTINUED:

                              BEN
          But you cannot control it. This is a danger-
          ous time for you, when you will be tempted by
          the dark side of the Force.

                              YODA
          Yes, yes. To Obi-Wan you listen. The cave.
          Remember your failure at the cave!

                              LUKE
          But I've learned so much since then. Master
          Yoda, I promise to return and finish what
          I've begun. You have my word.

                              BEN
          It is you and your abilities the Emperor
          wants. That is why your friends are made to
          suffer.

                              LUKE
          And that is why I have to go.

                              BEN
          Luke, I don't want to lose you to the Emperor
          the way I lost Vader.

                              LUKE
          You won't.

                              YODA
          Stopped they must be. On this all depends.
          Only a fully trained Jedi Knight with the
          Force as his ally will conquer Vader and his
          Emperor. If you end your training now, if you
          choose the quick and easy path, as Vader did,
          you will become an agent of evil.

                              BEN
          Patience.

                              LUKE
          And sacrifice Han and Leia?

                              YODA
          If you honor what they fight for . . . yes!

Luke is in great anguish. He struggles with the dilemma, a battle
raging in his mind.

                              BEN
          If you choose to face Vader, you will do it
          alone. I cannot interfere.

                              LUKE
          I understand. (he moves to his X-wing) Artoo,
          fire up the converters.

                                                    (CONTINUED)

CONTINUED:

Artoo whistles a happy reply.

                      BEN
        Luke, don't give in to hate — that leads to
        the dark side.

Luke nods and climbs into his ship.

                     YODA
        Strong is Vader. Mind what you have learned.
        Save you it can.

                     LUKE
        I will. And I'll return. I promise.

Artoo closes the cockpit. Ben and Yoda stand watching as the roar of
the engines and the wind engulfs them.

                     YODA
        (sighs) Told you, I did. Reckless is he. Now
        matters are worse.

                      BEN
        That boy is our last hope.

                     YODA
        (looks up) No. There is another.

EXT. SPACE — PLANET DAGOBAH

Luke's tiny X-wing rockets away from the green planet of Dagobah and
off into space.

INT. CLOUD CITY — LIVING QUARTERS — DAY

←Insert from page 88A for the Special Edition

Within the quarters assigned her on Cloud City, Leia paces in agita-
tion. She has changed from her cold-weather pants and jacket to a
lovely dress. Her hair is down, tied back with ribbons. She moves
from a large, open window and turns to see Han entering through the
doorway.

                     HAN
        The ship is almost finished. Two or three
        more things and we're in great shape.

                     LEIA
        The sooner the better. Something's wrong
        here. No one has seen or knows anything about
        Threepio. He's been gone too long to have
        gotten lost.

Han takes Leia by the shoulders and gently kisses her forehead.

                                      (CONTINUED)

CONTINUED:

                              HAN
          Relax. I'll talk to Lando and see what I can
          find out.

                              LEIA
          I don't trust Lando.

                              HAN
          Well, I don't trust him, either. But he is my
          friend. Besides, we'll soon be gone.

                              LEIA
          And then you're as good as gone, aren't you?

Not speaking, Han considers her words and gazes at her troubled face.

INT. CLOUD CITY — JUNK ROOM

The room is piled high with broken and discarded machine parts. Four
Ugnaughts, small hoglike creatures, separate the junk and throw some
pieces onto a conveyor belt which moves briskly toward a pit of
molten metal. Pieces of Threepio's golden body move down the belt.
Chewie enters the room and spots an Ugnaught picking up and inspect-
ing Threepio's head. The Wookiee barks a command, startling the
Ugnaught, then reaches to grab the head. But the Ugnaught tosses it
away from him to another Ugnaught. This game of keep-away goes on
until Threepio's head falls from their grip and bounces with a clang
onto the ground.

INT. CLOUD CITY — LIVING QUARTERS — DAY

The door zaps open. Chewbacca walks in, carrying a packing case of
Threepio, arms and legs hanging over the edges.

                              LEIA
          What happened?

Chewie sets the case on a table, grunting and groaning an explanation.

                              HAN
          Where? Found him in a junk pile?

                              LEIA
          Oh, what a mess. Chewie, do you think you can
          repair him?

The giant Wookiee studies the array of robot parts. He looks at the
princess and shrugs sadly.

                              HAN
          Lando's got people who can fix him.

                                                      (CONTINUED)

SPECIAL EDITION INSERT TO PAGE 87

EXT. BESPIN SURFACE — CLOUD CAR

A twin-pod cloud car flies forward away from the suspended Cloud City. Another cloud car banks along Cloud City's surface, between buildings and behind and around the tower room. Through a window, Leia can be seen pacing.

CONTINUED:

                    LEIA
        No, thanks.

There is a buzz and the door slides open, revealing Lando.

                    LANDO
        I'm sorry. Am I interrupting anything?

                    LEIA
        Not really.

                    LANDO
        You look absolutely beautiful. You truly
        belong here with us among the clouds.

                    LEIA
        (coolly) Thank you.

                    LANDO
        Will you join me for a little refreshment?

Han looks at Lando suspiciously, but Chewie barks at the mention of
food and licks his lips.

                    LANDO
        Everyone's invited, of course.

Leia takes Lando's proffered hand, and the group turns to go. Lando
spots Threepio's remains.

                    LANDO
        Having trouble with your droid?

Han and Leia exchange a quick glance.

                    HAN
        No. No problem. Why?

Han and Leia move arm in arm through the door, followed by Lando and
Chewie. The door slides closed behind them.

INT. CLOUD CITY — CORRIDOR — DAY

Leia walks between Han and Lando as Chewie follows a short distance
behind. Long shafts of light pour across the corridor between tall,
pure-white columns.

                    LANDO
        So, you see, since we're a small operation,
        we don't fall into the . . . uh . . . juris-
        diction of the Empire.

                    LEIA
        So you're part of the mining guild then?

CONTINUED:

                              LANDO
        No, not actually. Our operation is small
        enough not to be noticed . . . which is
        advantageous for everybody since our
        customers are anxious to avoid attracting
        attention to themselves.

The group walks into another corridor and heads for a huge doorway
at the far end.

                              HAN
        Aren't you afraid the Empire's going to find
        out about this little operation and shut you
        down?

                              LANDO
        That's always been a danger looming like a
        shadow over everything we've built here. But
        things have developed that will insure
        security. I've just made a deal that will keep
        the Empire out of here forever.

INT. CLOUD CITY — DINING ROOM

The mighty doors to the dining room slide open and the group enters.
At the far end of a huge banquet table sits Darth Vader. Standing at
his side and slightly behind him is Boba Fett, the bounty hunter.

Faster than the wink of an eye, Han draws his blaster and pops off a
couple of shots directly at Vader. The Dark Lord quickly raises his hand,
deflecting the bolts into one of the side walls, where they explode
harmlessly. Just as quickly, Han's weapon zips into Vader's hand. The
evil presence calmly places the gun on the table in front of him.

                            VADER
        We would be honored if you would join us.

Han gives Lando a mean look.

                            LANDO
        I had no choice. They arrived right before
        you did. I'm sorry.

                              HAN
        I'm sorry, too.

EXT. LUKE'S X-WING — BESPIN SYSTEM

Luke's X-wing races through thick clouds toward Cloud City.

INT. LUKE'S X-WING — COCKPIT

Luke is grim-faced as he pilots his course toward Bespin's shining
city. Artoo's beeps and whistles are transmitted onto the scope.

                    LUKE
          (into comlink) No, Threepio's with them.

Artoo whistles another worried inquiry.

                    LUKE
          (into comlink) Just hang on. We're almost there.

INT. CLOUD CITY — LARGE CELL

Chewbacca is in a Cloud City prison cell. The stark room is flooded
with hot light. To add to Chewie's misery, a high-pitched whistle
screeches loudly. Chewie is going mad. He hits the wall with his
giant fists as he paces back and forth across the cell floor. The
upper lights go off abruptly. The prisoner rubs his eyes and moves to
a wall, where he listens for a moment. Then, moaning to himself, he
moves to a platform where the disassembled pieces of Threepio lie. He
picks up the golden droid's head and meditates on it for a moment,
barking a few philosophical remarks. Chewie sticks the robot's head
on its torso and starts adjusting wires and circuits. Suddenly, the
lights in Threepio's eyes spark to life as Chewie touches two connec-
tors together. Threepio immediately begins to speak, but his voice is
so slow and so low as to be nearly unintelligible.

                    THREEPIO
          Mmm. Oh, my. Uh, I, uh — Take this off! I,
          uh, don't mean to intrude here. I, don't, no,
          no, no . . . Please don't get up. No!

Chewie looks at Threepio in bewilderment, then scratches his furry
head. He gets an idea and adjusts some connections, whereupon
Threepio immediately begins speaking normally.

                    THREEPIO
          Stormtroopers? Here? We're in danger. I must
          tell the others. Oh, no! I've been shot!

INT. CLOUD CITY — PRISON ENTRY AREA

Darth Vader strides through the room as two stormtroopers prepare an
elaborate torture mechanism. Han is strapped to a rack which tilts
forward onto the torture device. Vader activates the mechanism,
creating two bursts of sparks, one of which strikes Han in the face.

                                                    (CONTINUED)

CONTINUED:

The door opens, and Vader leaves the torture room just as Han screams a sharp, piercing cry of agony. Darth Vader moves to the holding chamber, where Lando and Boba Fett await him.

INT. CLOUD CITY — HOLDING CHAMBER

                    LANDO
        Lord Vader.

                    VADER
        (to Fett) You may take Captain Solo to Jabba
        the Hutt after I have Skywalker.

Han's screams filter through the torture room door.

                    BOBA FETT
        He's no good to me dead.

                    VADER
        He will not be permanently damaged.

                    LANDO
        Lord Vader, what about Leia and the Wookiee?

                    VADER
        They must never again leave this city.

                    LANDO
        That was never a condition of our agreement,
        nor was giving Han to this bounty hunter!

                    VADER
        Perhaps you think you're being treated
        unfairly.

                    LANDO
        No.

                    VADER
        Good. It would be unfortunate if I had to
        leave a garrison here.

Vader turns and sweeps into the elevator with Boba Fett. Lando walks swiftly down another corridor, muttering to himself.

                    LANDO
        This deal's getting worse all the time.

INT. CLOUD CITY — LARGE CELL

Chewie now has a little more of Threepio back together. One arm is connected, but the legs are yet to be attached. There is one small problem, however: It seems the Wookiee has managed to put the droid's head on backward.

                                        (CONTINUED)

CONTINUED:

                         THREEPIO
          Oh, yes, that's very good. I like that. Oh!
          Something's not right because now I can't
          see. Wait. Wait! Oh, my! What have you done?
          I'm backwards, you stupid furball. Only an
          overgrown mophead like you would be stupid
          enough . . .

Threepio is cut off in midsentence as Chewie angrily deactivates a
circuit and the droid shuts down. The Wookiee smells something and
sits up. The door to the chamber slides open and a ragged Han Solo
is shoved into the room by two stormtroopers. Barking his concern,
the huge Wookiee gives Han a big hug. Han is very pale, with dark
circles under his eyes.

                         HAN
          I feel terrible.

Chewie helps Han to a platform and then turns as the door slides
open revealing Leia. She, too, looks a little the worse for wear.
The troopers push her into the cell, and the door slides closed. She
moves to Han, who is lying on the platform, and kneels next to him,
gently stroking his head.

                         LEIA
          Why are they doing this?

                         HAN
          They never even asked me any questions.

The cell door slides open. Lando and two of his guards enter.

                         LEIA
          Lando.

                         HAN
          Get out of here, Lando!

                         LANDO
          Shut up and listen! Vader has agreed to turn
          Leia and Chewie over to me.

                         HAN
          Over to you?

                         LANDO
          They'll have to stay here, but at least
          they'll be safe.

                         LEIA
          What about Han?

                         LANDO
          Vader's giving him to the bounty hunter.

                         LEIA
          Vader wants us all dead.

                                        (CONTINUED)

CONTINUED:

                    LANDO
          He doesn't want you at all. He's after
          somebody called Skywalker.

                    HAN
          Luke?

                    LANDO
          Lord Vader has set a trap for him.

Leia's mind is racing.

                    LEIA
          And we're the bait.

                    LANDO
          Well, he's on his way.

Han's rage peaks.

                    HAN
          Perfect. You fixed us all pretty good, didn't
          you? (spits it out) My <u>friend</u>!

Han hauls off and punches Lando. The two friends are instantly
engaged in a frantic close-quarters fight. The guards hit Han with
their rifle butts and he flies across the room. Chewie growls and
starts for the guards. They point their laser weapons at the giant
Wookiee, but Lando stops them.

                    LANDO
          Stop! I've done all I can. I'm sorry I couldn't
          do better, but I have my own problems.

                    HAN
          Yeah, you're a real hero.

Lando and the guards leave. Han wipes the blood from his chin as
Leia and Chewie help him sit up.

                    LEIA
          (dabs at his wound) You certainly have a way
          with people.

INT. CLOUD CITY — CARBON-FREEZING CHAMBER

Four armor-suited stormtroopers stand at the ready in the large
chamber, which is filled with pipes and chemical tanks. In the
middle of the room is a round pit housing a hydraulic platform.
Darth Vader and Lando stand near the platform.

                    VADER
          This facility is crude, but it should be
          adequate to freeze Skywalker for his journey
          to the Emperor.

                                        (CONTINUED)

CONTINUED:

An Imperial soldier appears.

                    IMPERIAL SOLDIER
          Lord Vader, ship approaching. X-wing class.

                    VADER
          Good. Monitor Skywalker and allow him to land.

The soldier bows and leaves the chamber.

                    LANDO
          Lord Vader, we only use this facility for
          carbon freezing. If you put him in there, it
          might kill him.

                    VADER
          I do not want the Emperor's prize damaged. We
          will test it . . . on Captain Solo.

Lando's face registers dismay.

EXT. SPACE — BESPIN SYSTEM — LUKE'S X-WING

Luke's X-wing moves through the clouds as it nears the city.

INT. LUKE'S X-WING — COCKPIT

Encountering no city guards, Luke scans his display panels with
concern.

INT. CLOUD CITY — CARBON-FREEZING CHAMBER

There is great activity on the carbon-freezing platform. Six Ugnaughts
frantically prepare the chamber for use. A special coffinlike
container is put in place. With Boba Fett in the lead, a squad of six
stormtroopers brings in Han, Leia, and Chewie. Strapped to Chewie's
back, with only his head, torso, and one arm assembled, is Threepio.
Threepio's head faces the opposite direction from Chewie's and the
droid is constantly twisting around in a vain effort to see what is
happening. His one attached arm is animate and expressive, intermit-
tently pointing, gesturing, and covering his eyes. The remaining
pieces of his body are randomly bundled to the Wookiee's back so that
his legs and other arm stick out at odd angles from the pack.

                    THREEPIO
          If only you had attached my legs, I wouldn't
          be in this ridiculous position. Now,
          remember, Chewbacca, you have a responsi-
          bility to me, so don't do anything foolish.

                                              (CONTINUED)

CONTINUED:

                    HAN
        (to Lando) What's going on . . . buddy?

                    LANDO
        You're being put into carbon freeze.

Boba Fett moves away from the group to Darth Vader.

                    BOBA FETT
        What if he doesn't survive? He's worth a lot
        to me.

                    VADER
        The Empire will compensate you if he dies.
        Put him in!

Realizing what is about to happen, Chewie lets out a wild howl and
attacks the stormtroopers surrounding Han. Within seconds, other
Imperial reinforcements join the scuffle, clubbing the giant Wookiee
with their laser weapons. From the instant of Chewie's first move,
Threepio begins to scream in panic while he tries to protect himself
with his one arm.

                    THREEPIO
        Oh, no! No, no, no! Stop, Chewbacca,
        stop . . . !

The stormtroopers are about to bash Chewie in the face.

                    HAN
        Stop, Chewie, stop! Do you hear me? Stop!

                    THREEPIO
        Yes, stop, please! I'm not ready to die.

Han breaks away from his captors. Vader nods to the guards to let
him go and the pirate breaks up the fight.

                    HAN
        Chewie! Chewie, this won't help me. Hey!

Han gives the Wookiee a stern look.

                    HAN
        Save your strength. There'll be another time.
        The princess — you have to take care of her.
        You hear me?

Han winks at the Wookiee, who wails a doleful farewell.

In a flash the guards have slipped binders on Chewbacca, who is too
distraught to protest. Han turns to Princess Leia. They look sorrow-
fully at one another, then Han moves toward her and gives her a
final, passionate kiss.

                    LEIA
        I love you!

CONTINUED:

                              HAN
                    I know.

Tears roll down Leia's face as she watches the dashing pirate walk
to the hydraulic platform. Han looks one final time at his friends —
and then, suddenly, the platform drops. Chewie howls. Leia turns
away in agony. Lando winces in sorrow; it makes a life-changing
impression on him.

Instantly, fiery liquid begins to pour down in a shower of sparks
and fluid as great as any steel furnace. Holding Leia, Chewie half-
turns away from the sight, giving Threepio a view of the procedure.

                              THREEPIO
                    What . . . what's going on? Turn round,
                    Chewbacca, I can't see. Oh . . . they've
                    encased him in carbonite. He should be quite
                    well-protected — if he survives the freezing
                    process, that is.

Chewie is in no mood for technical discussions; he gives the droid
an angry glance and bark.

A huge mechanical tong lifts the steaming metal-encased space pirate
out of the vat and stands him on the platform. Some Ugnaughts rush
over and push the block over onto the platform. They slide the
coffinlike structure to the block and lift the metal block, placing
it inside. They then attach an electronic box onto the structure and
step away.

Lando kneels and adjusts some knobs, measuring the heat. He shakes
his head in relief.

                              VADER
                    Well, Calrissian, did he survive?

                              LANDO
                    Yes, he's alive. And in perfect hibernation.

Vader turns to Boba Fett.

                              VADER
                    He's all yours, bounty hunter. Reset the
                    chamber for Skywalker.

                              IMPERIAL OFFICER
                    Skywalker has just landed, my lord.

                              VADER
                    Good. See to it that he finds his way in
                    here. Calrissian, take the princess and the
                    Wookiee to my ship.

                              LANDO
                    You said they'd be left in the city under my
                    supervision.

                                                    (CONTINUED)

CONTINUED:

                              VADER
          I am altering the deal. Pray I don't alter it
          any further.

Lando's hand instinctively goes to his throat as he turns to Leia,
Chewie, and Threepio.

INT. CLOUD CITY — CORRIDOR — DAY

As Luke and Artoo move carefully down a deserted corridor, they hear
a group of people coming down a side hallway. Artoo lets out an
excited series of beeps and whistles. Luke glares at the tiny droid,
who stops in his tracks with a feeble squeak.

Boba Fett enters from a side hallway followed by two guards pushing
the floating, encased body of Han Solo. Two stormtroopers, who
follow, immediately spot Luke and open fire on him. The youth draws
his weapon and blasts the two troopers before they can get off a
second shot. The two guards whisk Han into another hallway as Fett
lowers his arm and fires a deadly laser at Luke, which explodes to
one side and tears up a huge chunk of wall.

Luke rushes to a side hallway, but by the time he reaches it, Fett,
Han, and the guards are gone. A thick metal door blocks the passage.
Luke turns to see Leia, Chewie, Threepio, and Lando being herded
down a second hallway by several other stormtroopers. Leia turns
just in time to see Luke.

                              LEIA
          Luke! Luke, don't — it's a trap! It's a trap!

Before she can finish, she is pulled through a doorway and disappears
from sight. Luke races after the group, leaving little Artoo trailing
behind.

INT. CLOUD CITY — ANTEROOM

Luke runs into an anteroom and stops to get his bearings. Leia and
the others are nowhere to be seen. Behind Luke, Artoo scoots down
the corridor toward the anteroom when suddenly a giant metal door
comes slamming down, cutting off Luke's exit. Several more doors
clang shut, echoing through the chamber.

INT. CLOUD CITY — HALLWAY LEADING TO ANTEROOM

Artoo stands with his nose pressed up against the giant metal door.
He whistles a long sigh of relief and, a little dazed, wanders off
in the other direction.

INT. CLOUD CITY — CARBON-FREEZING CHAMBER — ANTEROOM

Luke cautiously walks forward among hissing pipes and steam. Seeing an opening above him, he stops to look up. As he does, the platform he stands on begins to move.

INT. CLOUD CITY — CARBON-FREEZING CHAMBER

Luke rises into the chamber, borne by the platform. The room is deathly quiet. Very little steam escapes the pipes and no one else seems to be in the large room. Warily, Luke walks toward the stairway.

Steam begins to build up in the chamber. Looking up through the steam, Luke sees a dark figure standing on a walkway above him. Luke holsters his gun and moves up the stairs to face Vader. He feels confident, eager to engage his enemy.

                    VADER
          The Force is with you, young Skywalker. But
          you are not a Jedi yet.

Luke ignites his sword in answer. In an instant, Vader's own sword is lit. Luke lunges, but Vader repels the blow. Again Luke attacks, and the swords of the two combatants clash in battle.

INT. CLOUD CITY — CORRIDOR

Leia, Lando, and Chewie, with Threepio on his back, march along, guarded by six stormtroopers. The group reaches an intersection where Lobot and a dozen of Lando's guards stand at attention.

The guards immediately aim their weapons at the startled storm-troopers. Taking the stormtroopers' weapons from them, Lobot hands one to Leia and one to Lando.

                    LANDO
          Well done. Hold them in the security tower —
          and keep it quiet. Move.

As Lando's guards quickly march the stormtroopers away, Lando begins to undo Chewie's binding.

                    LEIA
          What do you think you're doing?

                    LANDO
          We're getting out of here.

                    THREEPIO
          I knew all along it had to be a mistake.

Chewie turns on Lando and starts to choke him.

                                        (CONTINUED)

CONTINUED:

                              LEIA
            Do you think that after what you did to Han
            we're going to trust you?

Lando tries to free himself from Chewie.

                              LANDO
            (choking) I had no choice . . .

Chewie barks ferociously.

                            THREEPIO
            (to Chewie) What are you doing? Trust him,
            trust him!

                              LEIA
            Oh, so we understand, don't we, Chewie? He
            had no choice.

                              LANDO
            I'm just trying to help . . .

                              LEIA
            We don't need any of your help.

                              LANDO
            (choking) H-a-a-a . . .

                              LEIA
            What?

                            THREEPIO
            It sounds like Han.

                              LANDO
            There's still a chance to save Han . . . I
            mean, at the East Platform . . .

                              LEIA
            Chewie.

Chewie finally releases Lando, who fights to get his breath back.

                            THREEPIO
            (to Lando) I'm terribly sorry about all this.
            After all, he's only a Wookiee.

EXT. CLOUD CITY — EAST LANDING PLATFORM — BOBA FETT'S SHIP

The two guards slide Han's encased body into an opening in the side
of the bounty hunter's ship. Boba Fett climbs aboard on a ladder
next to the side opening.

                            BOBA FETT
            Put Captain Solo in the cargo hold.

And with that, the door slams shut.

INT. CLOUD CITY — CORRIDOR

Lando, Leia, and Chewie run down a Cloud City corridor when suddenly
they spot Artoo who rushes toward them, beeping wildly.

                         THREEPIO
              Artoo! Artoo! Where have you been?

Chewie turns around to see the stubby droid, causing Threepio to be
spun out of sight of his friend.

                         THREEPIO
              Turn around, you woolly . . . ! (to Artoo)
              Hurry, hurry! We're trying to save Han from
              the bounty hunter!

Whistling frantically to Threepio, Artoo scoots along with the
racing group.

                         THREEPIO
              Well, at least you're still in one piece!
              Look what happened to me!

EXT. EAST LANDING PLATFORM — SIDE BAY

An elevator door slides open and Lando, Leia, and Chewbacca race for
a large bay overlooking the East Landing Platform.

Just as they arrive, Boba Fett's ship takes off against the cloudy
sunset sky.

In wild anguish, Chewie howls and starts firing at the ship.

                         THREEPIO
              Oh, no! Chewie, they're behind you!

A laser bolt explodes near the princess. Everyone turns to see what
Threepio has already spotted coming from the other direction: a
squad of stormtroopers running toward them. Artoo peeks out from the
elevator.

Leia and Chewbacca start firing at the troopers as Lando makes a
break for the elevator. Laser bolts continue to explode around the
princess and the Wookiee, but they refuse to budge. Lando sticks his
head out of the elevator and motions for the pair to run, but they
barely notice. They seem possessed, transported, as all the frustra-
tion of captivity and anger of loss pour out through their death-
dealing weapons.

But after a few moments, they begin to move through the rain of
laser fire toward the elevator. Once they are inside, the door slams
shut and the stormtroopers race forward.

INT. CLOUD CITY — CARBON-FREEZING CHAMBER

Luke and Vader are locked in combat on the platform overlooking the
chamber. Their swords clash, the platform sways. Luke aggressively
drives Vader back, forcing Vader to use defensive tactics.

                    VADER
          You have learned much, young one.

                    LUKE
          You'll find I'm full of surprises.

Vader makes two quick moves, hooking Luke's sword out of his hands
and sending it flying. Another lightning move at Luke's feet forces
the youth to jump back to protect himself. Losing his balance, Luke
rolls down the stairs to the circular carbon-freezing platform.
There he sprawls on the floor, surprised and shaken. Just in time he
looks up to see Vader, like a giant black bird, flying right at him.
Luke rolls away as Vader lands. Crouching, Luke keeps his gaze
steadily on his enemy.

                    VADER
          Your destiny lies with me, Skywalker. Obi-Wan
          knew this to be true.

                    LUKE
          No!

Behind Luke the hydraulic elevator cover has opened noiselessly. All
the while, Luke slowly, cautiously moves back, away from the Dark Lord.

Suddenly, Vader attacks so forcefully that Luke loses his balance
and falls back into the opening. There is a rumble, and in an
instant freezing steam rises to obscure Vader's vision. Vader turns
aside and deactivates his sword.

                    VADER
          All too easy. Perhaps you are not as strong
          as the Emperor thought.

Through the steam behind Vader something blurs upward. Liquid metal
begins to pour into the pit.

Vader turns around — and then looks up. He sees Luke, who has leaped
fifteen feet straight up and who now hangs from some hoses on the
carbonite outlet.

                    VADER
          Impressive . . . most impressive.

Luke jumps down to the platform where he is separated from Vader by
the steaming carbonite pit. He raises his hand. His sword, which had
fallen on another part of the platform, swiftly jumps into his
outstretched hand and is instantly ignited. Vader immediately lights
his sword as well.

                                        (CONTINUED)

CONTINUED:

                              VADER
          Obi-Wan has taught you well. You have controlled
          your fear . . . now release your anger.

Luke is more cautious, controlling his anger. He begins to retreat as
Vader goads him on. As Luke takes a defensive position, he realizes
he has been foolhardy. A quick sword exchange and Luke forces Vader
back. Another exchange and Vader retreats. Luke presses forward.

                              VADER
          Only your hatred can destroy me.

Breathing hard, Luke jumps in the air, turning a somersault over
Vader. He lands on the floor and slashes at Vader as the room
continues to fill up with steam.

Vader retreats before Luke's skillful sword. Vader blocks the sword,
but loses his balance and falls into the outer rim of pipes. The energy
Luke has used to stop Vader has brought him to the point of collapse.
Luke moves to the edge and looks down, but sees no sign of Vader. He
then deactivates his sword, hooks it on his belt, and lowers himself
into the pit.

INT. CLOUD CITY — TUNNEL AND REACTOR CONTROL ROOM

Moving through a tunnel-like entrance, Luke cautiously approaches
the reactor room. He ignites his sword and moves into the room and
toward a large window as Vader enters.

Luke raises his sword and moves forward to attack.

Behind Luke a large piece of machinery detaches itself from the wall and
comes smashing forward toward his back. Luke turns and cuts it in half
just as another machine comes hurtling at him. Using the Force, Luke
manages to deflect it and sends it flying as if it had hit an invisible
shield. A large pipe detaches and comes flying at Luke. He deflects it.
Sparking wires pull out of the walls and begin to whip at the youth.
Small tools and equipment come flying at him. Bombarded from all sides,
Luke does his best to deflect everything, but soon he is bloodied and
bruised. Finally, one machine glances off him and goes flying out the
large window. A fierce wind blows into the room, whipping everything
about and creating a horrendous noise. In the center of the room,
unmoving, stands the dark, rocklike figure of Vader.

A piece of machinery hits Luke and he is knocked out the window.

INT. GANTRY — OUTSIDE CONTROL ROOM — REACTOR SHAFT

Luke falls onto the gantry, rolls, and hangs over the edge, holding
his deactivated sword in hand. He puts the sword on his belt and
begins to scramble up.

INT. CLOUD CITY — CORRIDOR LEADING TO LANDING PLATFORM

Leia, Lando, Chewie, and the droids come round a corner and head for
the door to the landing platform. They glimpse the <u>Millennium Falcon</u>
for a moment before the door slams shut. The group ducks into an
alcove as stormtroopers arrive at the end of the corridor. The
troopers send a rain of laser bolts at the group. Chewie returns
their fire as Lando punches desperately at the door's control panel.

                    LANDO
          The security code has been changed!

                    THREEPIO
          Artoo, you can tell the computer to override
          the security system.

Threepio points to a computer socket on the control panel. Artoo
beeps and scoots toward it. Lando meanwhile has connected up to the
panel's intercom.

                    LANDO
               Attention! This is Lando Calrissian. The
               Empire has taken control of the city. I
               advise everyone to leave before more Imperial
               troops arrive.

←Replace with
insert from
page 104A
for the
Special
Edition

Artoo takes off a connector cover and sticks his computer arm into
the socket. Suddenly, a short beep turns into a wild scream. Artoo's
circuits light up, his head spins wildly, and smoke begins to seep
out underneath him. Quickly, Chewie pulls him away.

                    LANDO
               This way.

Lando, Leia, Artoo, and Chewie flee down the corridor. As he scoots
along with them, Artoo sends some angry beeps Threepio's way.

                    THREEPIO
               Don't blame me. I'm an interpreter. I'm not
               supposed to know a power socket from a
               computer terminal.

INT. CLOUD CITY — CORRIDOR

In a panic, Cloud City residents are trying to get out of the city.
Some carry boxes, others packages. They run, then change direction.
Some are shooting at stormtroopers, others simply try to hide.

Other stormtroopers pursue Lando, Leia, and Chewie who are firing
back at them. Artoo works on another door to the landing platform
while Threepio berates him for his seeming ineptitude.

                                              (CONTINUED)

SPECIAL EDITION INSERT TO PAGE 104

                            LANDO
        Attention! This is Lando Calrissian.

The citizens of Cloud City stop their activities to listen to Lando's announcement.

                            LANDO
        The Empire has taken control of the city. I advise everyone to
        leave before more Imperial troops arrive.

CONTINUED:

>   THREEPIO
>   What are you talking about? We're not inter-
>   ested in the hyperdrive on the Millennium
>   Falcon. It's fixed! Just open the door, you
>   stupid lump.

Chewie, Leia, and Lando retreat along the corridor. A triumphant
beep from Artoo — and the door snaps open.

>   THREEPIO
>   (to Artoo) I never doubted you for a second.
>   Wonderful!

Artoo lays down a cloud of fog, obscuring everything, as the group
dashes outside.

EXT. LANDING PLATFORM — CLOUD CITY — DUSK

They race for the Millennium Falcon as a battalion of stormtroopers
reaches the main door. Lando and Leia hold off the troops as the
droids get on board with Chewie. As Chewie bounds to the ship with
Threepio on his back, Threepio hits his head on the top of the ramp.

>   THREEPIO
>   Ouch! Oh! Ah! That hurt. Bend down, you
>   thoughtless . . . Ow!

Chewie starts up the ship. The giant engines begin to whine as Lando
and Leia race up the ramp under a hail of laser fire.

>   LANDO
>   Leia! Go!

INT. MILLENNIUM FALCON — CORRIDOR

Artoo drags the partially assembled Threepio down the corridor of
the Falcon.

>   THREEPIO
>   I thought that hairy beast would be the end
>   of me. Of course, I've looked better.

Artoo beeps understandingly.

INT. MILLENNIUM FALCON — COCKPIT

Chewie works the controls as Leia sits in Han's seat and Lando
watches over their shoulders. As Chewie pulls back on the throttle,
the ship begins to move.

EXT. CLOUD CITY — LANDING PLATFORM — DUSK

The Millennium Falcon lifts gracefully into the twilight sky and roars away from the city. Troops fire after it and TIE fighters take off in pursuit.

INT. GANTRY — OUTSIDE CONTROL ROOM — REACTOR SHAFT

Luke moves along the railing and up to the control room. Vader lunges at him and Luke immediately raises his lit sword to meet Vader's. Sparks fly as they duel, Vader gradually forcing Luke backward toward the gantry.

> VADER
> You are beaten. It is useless to resist. Don't
> let yourself be destroyed as Obi-Wan did.

Luke answers by rolling sideways and thrusting his sword at Vader so viciously that he nicks Vader on the shoulder. The black armor sparks and smokes and Vader seems to be hurt, but immediately recovers.

Luke backs off along the narrow end of the gantry as Vader comes at him, slashing at the young Jedi with his sword. Luke makes a quick move around the instrument complex attached to the end of the gantry. Vader's sword comes slashing down, cutting the complex loose; it begins to fall, then is caught by the rising wind and blown upward.

Luke glances at the instrument complex floating away. At that instant, Vader's sword comes down across Luke's right forearm, cutting off his hand and sending his sword flying. In great pain, Luke squeezes his forearm under his left armpit and moves back along the gantry to its extreme end. Vader follows. The wind subsides. Luke holds on. There is nowhere else to go.

> VADER
> There is no escape. Don't make me destroy you.
> You do not yet realize your importance. You
> have only begun to discover your power. Join
> me and I will complete your training. With our
> combined strength, we can end this destructive
> conflict and bring order to the galaxy.

> LUKE
> I'll never join you!

> VADER
> If you only knew the power of the dark side.
> Obi-Wan never told you what happened to your
> father.

> LUKE
> He told me enough! He told me you killed him.

(CONTINUED)

CONTINUED:

                    VADER
     No. I am your father.

Shocked, Luke looks at Vader in utter disbelief.

                    LUKE
     No. No. That's not true! That's impossible!

                    VADER
     Search your feelings. You know it to be true.

                    LUKE
     No! No! No!

                    VADER
     Luke. You can destroy the Emperor. He has
     foreseen this. It is your destiny. Join me,
     and together we can rule the galaxy as father
     and son. Come with me. It is the only way.

Vader puts away his sword and holds his hand out to Luke.

A calm comes over Luke, and he makes a decision. In the next instant
he steps off the gantry platform into space. The Dark Lord looks
over the platform and sees Luke falling far below. The wind begins
to blow at Vader's cape and the torrent finally forces him back,
away from the edge. The wind soon fades and the wounded Jedi begins
to drop fast, unable to grab on to anything to break his fall.

INT. REACTOR SHAFT

Suddenly, Luke is sucked into an exhaust pipe in the side of the
shaft. When Vader sees this, he turns and hurries off the platform.

INT. EXHAUST PIPE

Luke tumbles through the exhaust pipe.

He slides to the end of the slickly polished pipe and stops as his
feet hit a circular grill and knock it open. Luke claws at the
surface of the pipe, trying to keep from sliding out into space.

EXT. BOTTOM OF CLOUD CITY — WEATHER VANE — DUSK

Unable to hang onto the pipe, Luke tumbles out, emerging at the
undermost part of Cloud City. Reaching out desperately, he manages
to grab onto an electronic weather vane.

                    LUKE
     Ben . . . Ben, please!

(CONTINUED)

CONTINUED:

Luke tries to pull himself up on the weather vane but slips back down. He hooks one of his legs around the fragile instrument. All the while, a powerful current of air rushes out at him from the exhaust pipe.

                    LUKE
          Ben. Leia!

There is an ominous cracking sound from the base of the weather vane and a piece breaks off, falling into the clouds far below.

                    LUKE
          Hear me! Leia!

INT. MILLENNIUM FALCON — COCKPIT

Leia seems to be lost in a fog, her expression troubled. Chewie is busy operating the ship. Lando stands next to the Wookiee, watching a readout on the control panel.

                    LEIA
          Luke . . . We've got to go back.

Chewie growls in surprise.

                    LANDO
          What?

                    LEIA
          I know where Luke is.

                    LANDO
          But what about those fighters?

Chewie barks in agreement with Lando.

                    LEIA
          Chewie, just do it.

                    LANDO
          But what about Vader?

Chewie turns on Lando, the newcomer, with an ominous growl.

                    LANDO
          All right, all right, all right.

EXT. CLOUD CITY — MILLENNIUM FALCON — DUSK

The <u>Falcon</u> makes a graceful banking turn back toward Cloud City.

EXT. CLOUD CITY — LANDING PLATFORM

Vader enters the landing platform and watches as the speck that is
the <u>Falcon</u> disappears. The wind blows at his cape.

He turns to two aides who are standing near the entrance to the
landing platform.

                    VADER
          Bring my shuttle.

←Replace with insert from page 110A for the Special Edition

EXT. BOTTOM OF CLOUD CITY — WEATHER VANE

Nearly unconscious, Luke hangs upside-down on the weather vane as
his body shifts in the wind.

EXT. MILLENNIUM FALCON — BOTTOM OF CLOUD CITY

The <u>Falcon</u> dives to the underside of the floating city. Three TIE
fighters close in on the starship.

INT. MILLENNIUM FALCON — COCKPIT

Leia tries to remain calm.

                    LANDO
          (pointing out the cockpit window) Look,
          someone's up there.

                    LEIA
          It's Luke. Chewie, slow down. Slow down and
          we'll get under him. Lando, open the top hatch.

Lando rushes out of the cockpit.

EXT. BOTTOM OF CLOUD CITY — WEATHER VANE

Luke hangs by one arm from the crossbar of the weather vane. He
slips from the bar and grabs onto the pole of the vane as the <u>Falcon</u>
banks toward him. The <u>Falcon</u> positions itself under Luke as Lando
moves up through the opening of the hatch. Luke begins to slide and
finally falls from the vane into space.

←Insert from page 110A for the Special Edition

INT. MILLENNIUM FALCON — COCKPIT

Out the cockpit window, Leia sees Luke falling from the bottom of
the city. The ship gains on him.

                                              (CONTINUED)

CONTINUED:

                              LEIA
          Okay. Easy, Chewie.

The <u>Falcon</u> closes in on Luke.

EXT. BOTTOM OF CLOUD CITY

Three TIE fighters race toward the <u>Falcon</u>, firing away.

INT. MILLENNIUM FALCON — HATCH

The hatch pops open with a hiss of pressure. Lando reaches out to
help the battered warrior inside the ship.

INT. MILLENNIUM FALCON — COCKPIT

Flak bursts all around it as the <u>Falcon</u> banks away from the city.
Leia and Chewie struggle with the controls.

                            LEIA
          (into intercom) Lando?

                           LANDO
          (over intercom) Okay, let's go.

EXT. BOTTOM OF CLOUD CITY

The <u>Falcon</u> races away. It is closely followed by the three TIE
fighters, all of which keep up a heavy laser assault on the fleeing
starship.

INT. MILLENNIUM FALCON — COCKPIT

Explosions erupt all around the cockpit, buffeting the ship wildly.
Chewie howls as he frantically tries to control the ship.

Leia and Chewie turn to see Luke, bloody and battered, enter the
cockpit supported by Lando. Leia jumps up and hugs him while Chewie
barks in joyous relief.

                            LUKE
          Oh, Leia.

                           LANDO
          All right, Chewie. Let's go.

Leia helps Luke from the cockpit as another huge blast rocks the
ship.

SPECIAL EDITION INSERT TO PAGE 109

VADER
Alert the Star Destroyer to prepare for my arrival.

EXT. CLOUD CITY — LANDING PLATFORM

Darth Vader and his aides approach an Imperial shuttle parked on the landing platform.

SPECIAL EDITION INSERT TO PAGE 109

EXT. BESPIN — SPACE

The sun begins to show behind the planet Bespin. Three TIE fighters zoom in as Vader's shuttle approaches his Star Destroyer.

EXT. SPACE — CLOUD CITY — DAY

The <u>Falcon</u>, still followed by the three TIE fighters, races away from the cloud-covered city.

INT. MILLENNIUM FALCON — SLEEPING QUARTERS

Luke rests on a cot, his injured arm wrapped in a protective cuff. Leia gently wipes his face. The ship lurches again.

                    LEIA
          I'll be back.

She kisses him, then leaves the quarters.

←Insert from page 112A for the Special Edition.

INT. MILLENNIUM FALCON — COCKPIT

All over the ship muted alarm buzzers sound. Lando anxiously watches the flashing lights on the control panel and hurriedly adjusts some switches. Seated next to him, Chewie points out a new blip appearing on the panel. Leia, watching over their shoulders, recognizes the shape.

                    LEIA
          Star Destroyer.

                    LANDO
          All right, Chewie. Ready for lightspeed.

                    LEIA
          <u>If</u> your people fixed the hyperdrive.

Another explosion rocks the ship. Leia notices as a green light on the panel next to her flashes on.

                    LEIA
          All the coordinates are set. It's now or never.

Chewie barks in agreement.

                    LANDO
          Punch it!

The Wookiee shrugs and pulls back on the lightspeed throttle. The sound of the ion engine changes . . . it is winding up. Faces are tense, expectant. But nothing happens, and the engine goes off. Chewie lets out a frustrated howl. The flak still violently rocks the ship.

                    LANDO
          They told me they fixed it. I trusted them to
          fix it. It's not my fault!

Chewie gets up from his chair and starts out of the cockpit. He gives Lando an angry shove as he storms past him.

EXT. SPACE

In the distance the TIE fighters continue their chase, still
shooting lasers. Vader's Star Destroyer moves behind them, deter-
minedly following the <u>Falcon</u>.

INT. VADER'S STAR DESTROYER — BRIDGE

Vader stands on the bridge looking out the window as Admiral Piett
approaches him.

                    PIETT
          They'll be in range of our tractor beam in
          moments, Lord.

                    VADER
          Did your men deactivate the hyperdrive on the
          <u>Millennium Falcon</u>?

                    PIETT
          Yes, my lord.

                    VADER
          Good. Prepare the boarding party and set your
          weapons for stun.

                    PIETT
          Yes, my lord.

INT. MILLENNIUM FALCON — HOLD

Beeping while he works, Artoo is busy connecting some wires to
Threepio who now has one leg attached.

Chewie enters through the doorway, grunting to himself.

                    THREEPIO
          Noisy brute. Why don't we just go into light-
          speed?

Artoo beeps in response.

                    THREEPIO
          We can't? How would you know the hyperdrive
          is deactivated?

Artoo whistles knowingly.

                    THREEPIO
          The city's central computer told you? Artoo-
          Detoo, you know better than to trust a
          strange computer. Ouch! Pay attention to what
          you're doing!

                                        (CONTINUED)

SPECIAL EDITION INSERT TO PAGE 111

INT. STAR DESTROYER — HANGAR BAY

Technicians oversee Vader's shuttle as it lands in the Star Destroyer's hangar bay. Armed Imperial stormtroopers stand close by. The shuttle's ramp lowers, and Darth Vader exits, walking toward two lines of officers standing at attention.

CONTINUED:

Chewie is in the pit. He is trying to loosen something with an enormous wrench. Frustrated, he uses the wrench like a club and hits the panel . . .

INT. MILLENNIUM FALCON — COCKPIT

Leia and Lando, seated in front of the control panel, are suddenly sprayed by a shower of sparks.

INT. VADER'S STAR DESTROYER — BRIDGE

Vader stands on the bridge, watching as the <u>Millennium Falcon</u> is chased by the TIE fighters. As his Destroyer draws nearer, Vader's breathing gets slightly faster.

             VADER
   Luke.

INT. MILLENNIUM FALCON — SLEEPING QUARTERS

Luke realizes that Vader's ship is very near. He feels resigned to his fate. He senses that he is beaten, more emotionally than physically.

             LUKE
   Father.

INT. VADER'S STAR DESTROYER — BRIDGE

             VADER
   Son, come with me.

INT. MILLENNIUM FALCON — SLEEPING QUARTERS

             LUKE
   (moaning) Ben, why didn't you tell me?

INT. MILLENNIUM FALCON — COCKPIT

Lando and Leia are at the controls of the <u>Falcon</u>. Meanwhile, in the ship's hold, Chewie continues to work frantically on the hyperdrive mechanism.

             LANDO
   (into intercom) Chewie!

EXT. SPACE

The <u>Falcon</u> races through space followed very closely by the TIE
fighters and the huge Imperial Star Destroyer.

INT. MILLENNIUM FALCON — COCKPIT

Luke enters the cockpit and looks out the window. He is almost
unconscious with pain and depression.

                         LUKE
          It's Vader.

INT. VADER'S STAR DESTROYER — BRIDGE

                         VADER
          Luke . . . it is your destiny.

INT. MILLENNIUM FALCON — COCKPIT

                         LUKE
          Ben, why didn't you tell me?

INT. VADER'S STAR DESTROYER — BRIDGE

                         PIETT
          Alert all commands. Ready for the tractor beam.

INT. MILLENNIUM FALCON — HOLD

Artoo races to a control panel and starts working on a circuit
board. Furious, Threepio stands on one leg, yelling.

                         THREEPIO
          Artoo, come back at once! You haven't
          finished with me yet! You don't know how to
          fix the hyperdrive. Chewbacca can do it. I'm
          standing here in pieces, and you're having
          delusions of grandeur!

Artoo moves a circuit on a control panel. Suddenly, the control
panel lights up.

INT. MILLENNIUM FALCON — COCKPIT

Leia and Lando are thrown back into their seats as the Millennium
Falcon unexpectedly shoots into hyperdrive.

INT. MILLENNIUM FALCON — HOLD

The ship tilts up and Artoo topples into the pit on top of Chewie.

                    THREEPIO
          Oh, you did it!

EXT. SPACE

The Falcon soars into infinity and away from the huge Star
Destroyer, which seems, by contrast, to stand still.

INT. VADER'S STAR DESTROYER — BRIDGE

Admiral Piett and another captain glance at Vader in terror. Vader
turns slowly and walks off the bridge, his hands held behind his
back in a contemplative gesture.

EXT. SPACE — REBEL STAR CRUISER

The Millennium Falcon is attached to a huge Rebel cruiser by a
docking tube. Rebel fighters move about the giant cruiser, and a
Rebel transport ship hovers near the fleet.

INT. MILLENNIUM FALCON — COCKPIT

Lando sits in the pilot's seat as he talks into the comlink. Chewie
busily throws a variety of switches in preparation for takeoff.

                    LANDO
          (into comlink) Luke, we're ready for takeoff.

                    LUKE
          (over comlink) Good luck, Lando.

                    LANDO
          (into comlink) When we find Jabba the Hutt
          and that bounty hunter, we'll contact you.

INT. STAR CRUISER — MEDICAL CENTER

Luke speaks into the comlink as a medical droid works on his hand.
Leia stands near him while Threepio and Artoo look out the window.

>   LUKE
>   (into comlink) I'll meet you at the
>   rendezvous point on Tatooine.

INT. MILLENNIUM FALCON — COCKPIT

>   LANDO
>   (into comlink) Princess, we'll find Han. I
>   promise.

INT. STAR CRUISER — MEDICAL CENTER

>   LUKE
>   (into comlink) Chewie, I'll be waiting for
>   your signal.

Chewie's wail comes over the comlink.

>   LUKE
>   (into comlink) Take care, you two. May the
>   Force be with you.

Luke looks down at his hand. A metalized type of bandage has been
wrapped around his wrist. The medical droid makes some adjustments
in a tiny electronic unit, then pricks each one of Luke's fingers.

>   LUKE
>   Ow!

Luke wriggles his fingers, makes a fist, and relaxes it. His hand is
completely functional.

He gets up and walks over to Leia. There is a new bond between them, a
new understanding. Leia is thinking about Han; Luke is thinking about
his uncertain and newly complicated future. Together they stand at the
large window of the medical center looking out on the Rebel Star Cruiser
and a dense, luminous galaxy swirling in space. Luke puts his arm around
Leia. The droids stand next to them, and Threepio moves closer to Artoo,
putting his arm on him. The group watches as the <u>Millennium Falcon</u> moves
into view, makes a turn, and zooms away into space.

EXT. SPACE — REBEL STAR CRUISER

While Luke, Leia, and the droids stand, looking out the window of
the star cruiser, two escort fighters join the large ship. Slowly,
the cruiser turns and moves away into space.

DISSOLVE TO:

EXT. GALAXY—SPACE

END CREDITS FADE IN AND OUT OVER BACKGROUND

THE END